Releasing Emotional Baggage

Overcoming the

Storms & Trials

of life and...

Awakening to a new Reality!

ISBN # 978-0-9720398-9-5

Other Books by Mia Y. Merritt:
Prosperity is Your Birthright!
Prosperity is Your Birthright Workbook
Destined for Great Things!
Destined for Great Things Workbook
Words of Inspiration: Golden Nuggets for the Wise at Heart
Life After High School
Life After High School Workbook

Library of Congress Cataloging
in-Publication Data

Merritt, Mia

First Printing 2011
Printed in the U.S.A.

DEDICATION

This book is dedicated to every man and woman who have gone through sexual molestation, rape, abandonment, rejection, physical/verbal/emotional abuse, heartbreaks, domestic violence, mistreatment, divorce, grief, or been being cheated on. Understand that the trials and struggles, the hardships and difficulties, even the victories and triumphs in your life were designed to make you stronger. In this thing called life, you will not escape the bad times, but there will be many good times. Your life will not always be good nor will it always be bad. There will be some mountaintop experiences and there will be some wilderness and valley experiences. What matters is how you deal with whatever comes your way; what is produced in you; the wisdom you acquire from having endured such circumstances. This book is dedicated to you because God knows all about what you have endured, what you may be going through and what waits for you in distance. He has already decreed that you are victorious and you will overcome every obstacle and challenge, just as you have in the past. You are more than a conqueror. This book is for you!

In memory of my daughter,
Stephanie Leanne Sanders

You turned fourteen years old on
May 26, 2011.
I never stop thinking about you.

Your Spirit will always remain alive
in my heart and I will forever cherish
the 93 days we spent
together.

God Bless Your Little Soul!

INTRODUCTION

We all have some emotional baggage which has resulted because of the things we have gone through in life. In this book, emotional baggage is referred to as leftover feelings resulting from emotional pain and psychological bruises from the past. Baggage usually causes bitterness, fear, doubt, suspicion, distrust, withdrawal, hesitation, or failure to love or be loved; and these feelings are hidden behind a big invisible wall that you walk around with to protect yourself from getting hurt again. When we hear the term 'emotional baggage' we automatically think of women, but men carry emotional baggage around as well. When baggage has not been appropriately dealt with, it seeps out little by little and sabotages new relationships that would otherwise have long-term potential.

In order to walk in liberty, live in harmony and exude the peace and joy of the Lord, we have to get free! Your painful past events must be dealt with head on and then released. This is called getting delivered. Only you know if you still have baggage that is causing frustration in your life. If there are things that have happened in your past that causes shame, guilt, anger, bitterness or resentment to emerge inside you when you think about them, then you are not delivered. Deliverance means that the memories of those painful events no longer haunt you or cause you to feel bad. This book is written to help you get delivered from those past emotions that keep you in mental bondage. You are not less of a person because of those experiences; if anything, consider yourself privileged that God chose you because He knew that you would endure and overcome them. There is no glory without a story. Where there is no test, there is no testimony.

TABLE OF CONTENTS

Chapter 1

Identifying Emotional Baggage

History is what happened in the past. Baggage is comprised of all the emotions and feelings that were left behind from those negative, painful or shameful events that happened in the past. Life's experiences change us for better or for worse. Almost everyone, both men and women have endured some kind of emotional pain; but there are people who have endured significantly more than others to the point that it affects relationships in almost every area of their lives. The residue from their past spills over into their relationships, friendships, associations, interactions with coworkers, and often clouds their perception about things and people. Leftover feelings resulting from emotional pain and psychological bruising of your past create baggage. This baggage usually causes bitterness, fear, doubt, suspicion, distrust withdrawal, hesitation, or failure to love or be loved; and these feelings are hidden behind a big invisible wall that you walk around with to protect yourself. Unfortunately, people with baggage bring their bags (leftover feelings) with them into each new

1

relationship with the opposite sex. In the beginning of a new relationship, things appear to be good, as it always does, but as time progresses, challenging situations emerge. Arguments develop. The way in which the arguments are dealt with, the words that are said, and the reactions made while dealing with the issues, determine if it is the baggage that has surfaced or not. When emotional baggage runs deep, its effect sabotages relationships that would otherwise have had long term potential, because residue from the past hurt rises up and makes its presence known. The tricky thing about emotional baggage is that most people do not realize that they are still carrying it around within them, even after it has revealed itself time and time again in relationships. When the items in your bags start falling out, meaning that pain from past memories emerge again, they begin slowly but surely undermining any good that would come out of the new relationship, ultimately destroying it. When you do not realize what has happened, you move on to the next relationship with heavier baggage (residue from the last relationship) and the cycle repeats itself again.

It is always a good idea to reflect over your life and determine whether any emotional baggage has contributed to failure in past relationships. The baggage may even be causing conflict in current relationships. Reflect. I know that every bad thing that happened was or is not your fault, but look beyond the surface and go to the root cause of things that happened, not just in past personal relationships, but in family quarrels, situations on the job, continuous altercations with others, etc. What was the root cause of the problem? Did any situation get out of control? If so, why? Who overreacted? Who remained calm or at least tried to remain calm? How did you respond to the situation? What kind of thoughts do you remember thinking during those incidents? If you notice that the same pattern of problems arise in most or all of your relationships, then you need to take a closer look at any negative emotions and fears that you may be clinging to. If you can look back and see some baggage that emerged because of what you inwardly feared, then the time is right now to face those painful hurts of the past and deal with them appropriately if you desire to move forward positively towards healthy future relationships. Even if it has been years or even decades since the painful events occurred, it is never too late for deliverance and healing. The only factor that all of your failed relationships have in common, is YOU. Therefore you must accept the fact that the only way to stop the sabotaging patterns from presenting themselves in yet more relationships lies within you.

3

In order to get a hold of the emotional baggage that resurfaces over and over in interactions and relationships with people, you must recognize the emotional baggage that you have and admit that you have it. Recognition is the first step. Otherwise the old baggage will remain and new baggage will be added to it each time you experience a hurt that is not resolved or dealt with properly. Those unresolved feelings are internalized, which causes mental anguish and emotional turmoil inside of you. This suppression adds to the layers of hurt you already have and creates a heavier burden; and the hurt seeps out frequently because there has been no release or eradication of it. The baggage does not want to be confined. It wants expression. Therefore, it will find a way to get out. It carries itself into relationship after relationship, and the same fears and negative emotions trigger irrational thoughts and unreasonable behaviors that contribute to the ultimate decline of the relationship. This is a cycle that you are unable to escape from in your romantic life until the root causes of your baggage is dealt with. Until then, you will go from person to person thinking that if you find the right person to love you, they will take all the hurt and pain away. This is a delusion.

Women tend to carry emotional baggage around more often than men. But there are many men who have experienced deep psychological bruising and traumatic pain just as women have. However, most men are less inclined to talk about their past pain and current issues, which creates a much deeper suppression. They tend to think that it is not "manly" or "masculine" to do that. They think it is a sign of weakness, but in actuality, it is a sign of strength and understanding of the importance of   release.   This suppression   contributes   to deterioration in their relationships with women as well because just like women, the baggage of men starts falling out too. There are men out there with so many issues. They are moody, emotionally unstable, and simply cannot maintain a healthy relationship with a woman. This is because of all the emotional baggage in their life that has   not   been   dealt   with.   Oftentimes   men overcompensate   for   their   past   hurt   by   being controlling, cold and hard. This is a coping mechanism that they think will prevent them from getting hurt by another woman again. This too is a delusion. People are walking around with deep hurt, emotional scars and psychological bruising everyday stemming from things   that   have   happened   in   their   childhood, adulthood, past relationships, and even stemming back from their toddler ages. Many are experiencing things right now. They put a smile on their faces and tuck their hurt away into the corners and crevices of their soul while trying to keep from having to face the pain that has taken residence within them. This is why it is so important to be kind to people. You never know what others may be going through. Your smile or kind word can be just enough to help them make it through another day. Unless past issues are dealt with head on, they will never disappear, but will raise their ugly head making themselves known at the most inopportune times in a person's life.

Getting to the root cause of things is the only way that a situation can be effectively dealt with or eradicated. We often look at symptoms and treat those symptoms instead of going deeper to discover the cause of the symptoms. The purpose of a symptom is to inform you that there is an underlying problem somewhere. It is to serve as a sign only. Webster's dictionary defines the word symptom as the following:

1. A physical or mental feature that is regarded as indicating a condition or disease

2. A sign of the existence of something, i.e. an undesirable situation.

Notice that both definitions have the words, *indication* and *sign*, meaning that a symptom only serves to inform you that something bad lies beneath the surface. That is why pain is often good because it tells you that something is wrong and you can get help. If you never go beyond the surface to uncover what is there, you will never get to the root. If a person is constantly suffering from headaches and all they do is take Excedrin or Tylenol each time a headache comes on, then they are only treating the symptom, not the cause. A brain tumor or aneurism could be causing the headaches and if not treated in time, could be deadly. When it comes to emotional baggage, in order to get to the root, you must go within to the cause of why you react, behave, explode, experience or gravitate to certain things and feelings the way you do. Everything has a root cause and as long as the root remains, the fruit will remain. Look at it this way: A seed is planted. Years later there is a big tree, which continues to grow and gets larger and larger each year. But someone decides that the tree is no longer needed, so the decision is made to cut it down; but the only thing that is cut are branches and the bark. On the surface, all looks well. The tree is gone. But in a couple of months, something begins to break forth from the ground in the very spot where the tree used to be. In a couple of years, there is another tree in that spot. It too is cut down, but in a few more years, another tree has risen up in the same spot where the original tree was. Why is this? Because the root was never destroyed. As long as there is a root, there will always be fruit that rises up over time until the entire root has been pulled

7

up. This is why in biblical days when the Israelites would invade a city that had been promised to them, God would tell them to kill everyone - the men, women, *and* the children. Oh, how I used to think that was so cruel, but I understand now that God knew and knows the importance of entirely eradicating and wiping out that which is corrupt or not good. Had the Israelites allowed the women and children to remain, and killed the men only, the women, although weak and helpless, would have intermarried the Israelite men and the children would have grown up and intermarried the Israelite children. The seed of revenge, bitterness and anger that was planted and rooted in the women and passed on to the children would have eventually risen up. The children who would become adults would at some point attack, take over, and kill the Israelites in order to avenge the death of their fathers. If you want to get rid of something entirely, you must kill the root, which is oftentimes not easy because the very word "root" means that something is deep. It has gone downward. This is why when bad things happen to you, you must not allow the thought of that thing to fester. You must not constantly think about it and allow it to dominate your mind because what will happen is that it will sink down into your thoughts, then will pass over into your subconscious mind, then will get all into your spirit and soul and ultimately will change who you are.

When this happens, that negative seed has taken root in you. It has gone down deep into you and it will take a whole lot of work to pull it completely out of you. Healing of the soul, the spirit, and the mind needs to take place. You must not allow negativity to consume you. It is imperative that you learn to let things go. Remember that fibroids, cancer, ulcers, tumors, headaches, body aches and nervous breakdowns all have a root cause.

In the book of Jeremiah chapter 1:10, God said the following words to Jeremiah the Prophet: *...I have this day set thee over the nations and over the kingdoms, to root out, and to pull down, and to destroy, and to throw down, to build, and to plant.* We have this same authority. You can go up into the spirit realm, speak boldly and authoritatively to every principality, power, ruler of the darkness of this world and spiritual wickedness in high places and tell them what to do. Command them to loose whatever it is that you feel the powers of darkness have taken hold of: your health, your finances, your peace of mind, your children's thoughts, your spouse, your job, etc. Then, you can command them to restore back to you seven-fold what has been taken. Use your spiritual authority to strip them of their power. Just say, *I strip you of your power. I render your assignment against me null and void. I loose confusion over you.* Speak to the residue from their assignment against you and decree

9

that it shall not rise up a second time! You can use the power and spiritual authority you have to command, decree, affirm, proclaim, pronounce, uproot, pull down, destroy and throw down. Then, you can build and plant by the words of your mouth. This is the same power that God gave to Jeremiah. You have it too.

It is the same with emotional baggage. You have got to face it head on, get to the root and destroy it. In this world, there are so many symptoms and all we do is treat the symptoms, which is only a temporary fix, but the underling problem never goes away. Depression is a symptom. Homosexuality is a symptom. Prostitution is a symptom. Drug addiction, Schizophrenia, nervous breakdowns, and abuse of any kind are also all symptoms. You must know however, that for every problem there is a solution and as a child of God, your words, your prayers, your fasting and your study are your most valuable weapons against the enemy!

Do not be fooled into believing that when you find someone to completely accept and love you that you will be complete. You will never find that person because he or she does not exist. Everything is found on the inside of you. If you do not deal with your baggage, your relationships will not last because of the weight that you are putting on other people to give you the things that you should find within yourself. It becomes too much for anyone else to bear, and it is not fair to the other person. You are not an incomplete person looking for someone to complete you. You are already whole and complete in Christ. He is the finished work of the cross and He endured all your physical and emotional pain, so why are you still holding on to it? What complete man wants an incomplete woman? What complete woman wants an incomplete man? Even the incomplete man wants a complete woman. No man wants a woman who is too needy, too emotionally clingy, or has too much baggage. Get yourself together before embarking upon another relationship. That way, when God blesses you with a worthy person, you will bring value into their life. You will be an asset and not a liability or emotional burden. The relationship will be reciprocal and can learn and grow. Deal with YOU first. Spend time with God and ask for inner healing and deliverance so that when you are ready for a new relationship, it will be a healthy one. There is no void that God can not fill to make you whole again.

Until you love, understand, forgive and accept yourself for who you truly are, flaws and all, you will always pursue external relationships with hopes of finding love and acceptance from other people; but you can only find that love and acceptance inside of you. Too many people look for happiness and joy outside of themselves, but external conditions and people can never fill a void that you may feel. Nothing outside of you can make you happy. Everything you need is found within the reservoir of your soul. The kingdom of heaven is within you. The spirit of God is within you. Stop looking for Mr. or Mrs. Right to make you happy. Stop looking in the malls for happiness. Clothes, shoes, purses and jewelry can not make you happy or fill your void. Stop looking up at the sky for God. God is closer to you than the air that you breathe. Find God within you.

CAUSES OF EMOTIONAL BAGGAGE

Emotional baggage can be caused by so many different things including sexual molestation, rape, abandonment, rejection, physical/verbal/emotional abuse, heartbreaks, domestic violence, mistreatment, divorce, grief, being cheated on, etc. The cause of emotional baggage and pain is not really the main issue, however. The main factor, which is the key to proper healing, is how you handle what has happened to you. When you choose to try and forget about the past by not talking about it, and try to live life as though those horrible things never happened, you will never truly be free nor can you ever be until those issues are effectively dealt with. Facing your past changes your future positively. Allow yourself to learn from your painful experiences and find the good that emerged from each of them. I know that something like a rape or being molested, cheated on, or losing a loved one to death is very difficult to find good in, but if your faith made you stronger as a result of what happened to you, or you were able to help another person find deliverance by sharing your experience with them; or if you were able to help put the person in prison before he raped or molested again, then those are some good things that emerged from bad situations. Trust me, if you look hard enough with an open mind and heart, you will find something good out of EVERY negative experience or situation. Weak people blame God for bad things. God does not send bad things upon us. He created the law of cause and effect and this law carries out results that correspond with their initial causes. Remember, there is always a root cause for everything.

If there is no release of emotional baggage, it will manifest in one way or another. Seeping out in relationships is only one way that baggage shows its ugly head, but if there is no outlet there (because there may not be a relationship) then it will manifest in the body in the form of disease. People do not get sick because of what they eat; they get sick because of what is eating them. Just because you can not physically see something, does not mean does not exist. You can not see hurt, pain, disappointment, shame, guilt, bitterness or unforgiveness, but they are very real and they do have an existence. You can see and feel their effects in a person's life. You cannot see love, joy, peace, harmony, and contentment, but you can see their effects in people's lives. Everything has two births, first an invisible creation, then the physical manifestation. When the physical manifestations of love, joy, peace, harmony, and contentment appear, they are revealed in the form good health, peace and harmony in people's lives. There is wholeness in spirit, mind, body and soul when there is love, peace and harmony. When the physical manifestations of unforgiveness, bitterness, anger, guilt and shame appear, they reveal themselves in the form of tumors, ulcers, cancers, fibroids, migraines, nightmares, etc. It is detrimental to your mental and physical health to release negative emotions. Let go of that emotional baggage.

THE EFFECTS OF UNFORGIVENESS

Unforgiveness is the greatest block to healing. Without forgiving, total healing is impossible. Forgiveness is the foundation upon which healing emerges. The inability to forgive has been the most widespread sin that blocks a deliverance from occurring. Unforgiveness is one of the primary tools that Satan uses to gain a stronghold into a believer's life. He is very strategic. He works somewhat like this: You love the Lord. Your life is predicated upon praise, worship, fasting and loving your sisters and brothers in Christ. Satan has to stop your effectiveness because

14

you are advancing the kingdom of God too much. He enters into a person and uses them to offend and hurt you deeply. The seed of hurt, disappointment and anger has now been planted in you. The offense they did to you seems too much to forgive, so you hold on to the bitterness and unforgiveness. Now it becomes a part of you. Your prayers are now hindered. You are no longer as effective in the spirit as you once were, but you are trying to move forward in the manner you were prior to the hurt, but you can't because unforgiveness has taken root in you and until you deal with the issue and sincerely forgive, you will never be as effective in the spirit as you once were.

Unforgiveness is one of the most prolific causes for disease. It is a very powerful emotion, if not the most powerful one next to love. Spiritually, it keeps a person in bondage. It is a stronghold, having a very "strong" "hold" on a person. One is never truly free, nor can they walk in total liberty so long as they are holding unforgiveness in their heart toward anybody. Unforgiveness is one of Satan's most powerful tools, which is why he continues telling you lies so that you will never want to release it. He tells you things like: *You can not let what he/she did go; If you forgive him or her, then you are a fool; If you forgive them, then you are giving the green light for them to hurt you again; Do not ever forgive them; Make them hurt the way they hurt you, etc.* Satan has a bag of lies that he

15

feeds you with so you will continue holding on to the unforgiveness; but the truth is that forgiveness frees you. It does not hurt the other person, it only hurts you! After a while, the person who hurt you will forgive themselves and they will move on while you are still harboring on to what they did to you. Forgiveness does not have to mean reconciliation; it means release. It is one-sided. You do not need the other person in order to forgive them. You simply release what they did from your consciousness. When you think about what they did and you no longer want them to pay for it, then you know that you have released it. It may take a while for the hurt to go away, but if you choose not to harbor on it, and you dismiss the negative thought about it every time it comes to your mind, then in time, it will no longer have a negative effect on you. Forgiveness is simply a decision made to let it go. It is as easy as that. Forgiveness is not as hard as the devil makes it seem.

Unforgiveness is one of the heaviest weights in your emotional baggage bag. When you finally get rid of it, you feel so much lighter. You are a happier and healthier person. It feels so good to live in peace with others and go forward in the joy and freedom of the Lord. Forgiveness brings restoration, healing, and peace.

HOW TO EMPTY YOUR EMOTIONAL BAGGAGE

You have to release your emotional baggage in order to move forward and begin cultivating healthy relationships, but you have to want to be healed, and it will take some sacrifice and effort on your part. Satan will not make it easy. He wants you bound up, yoked up and held captive by shame, deep hurt, anger, bitterness, regret, guilt, etc. Below are some things that you can do to begin the process of forgiveness and emotional healing:

- Talk to someone about what happened to you. Explain how you felt then, how you feel about it now, and how you will move forward in the future in spite of what happened in the past. A therapist, counselor, psychologist, friend, priest, pastor, or someone that you trust can help with this. When you release it by talking about it, you will feel better because you then have less to carry around. When you hold on to it and refuse to discuss it or release it, you continue to feel weighted down with the burden of that heavy baggage in your soul.

- Forgive yourself. If you don't forgive yourself, you won't forgive others. You have to begin to forgive yourself for everything that happened. This is the foundation upon which everything else will be built. Healing will never happen if you don't forgive yourself.

- When facing the events that caused you baggage, you must allow yourself to "feel" the pain from those emotions and then deal with that pain appropriately: anger, bitterness, sadness, grief, fear, frustration, guilt, shame, rejection, sorrow etc. Coming to terms with your past is not easy, but it is necessary in order for you to move on. It is like going through the fire but coming out as pure gold!

- Love yourself and believe that in spite of what happened to you, you are still worthy of happiness, love, blessings, peace and joy in your life. God knows all about what happened to you and He knows that you are strong enough to overcome it; otherwise He would not have allowed it.

- Allow yourself to acknowledge that your past does not determine your future. The past is gone. There is no bringing it back no matter how hard you try. Therefore, look forward to the future. Joy, peace, harmony and blessings

18

are waiting for you because you deserve to possess them.

- Release all of the emotional hurt, anger, bitterness and fears that are weighing you down by speaking directly to them. Say, *"You will no longer haunt me or have a stronghold over my life. I release all negative feelings connected to my past and I move forward with joy, peace, and possibilities toward my future."*

- Accept and embrace the new person that you are becoming and live each day with the expectation of good. Walk in receptivity to great things and do not be surprised when great things happen for you. You get what you prepare for, so start now to prepare for God's blessings.

- Keep a journal and write your feelings down in the same way you would talk to an old friend about it.

As you have learned, emotional baggage does sabotage relationships. You are an evolving being and you are constantly progressing and becoming a new person. It is only through experiences that you become well-rounded and strong.

As I close this chapter, I want you to know beyond a shadow of a doubt that you are a very special person. Do not doubt it for a minute! You are valuable and precious in God's sight. He knows what He placed inside of you and it is valuable. When God speaks to you, He does it in a variety of ways. Right now, He speaks to you from the pages of this book. It is not by accident that you are reading these words. They are just for YOU. Your past does not matter. What matters is that you forgive everything and everyone who hurt you and move forward with great expectations. Below are some scriptures to encourage you and help you heal.

SCRIPTURAL NUGGETS

❖ **Mark 11:25**: And when ye stand praying, forgive if ye have ought against any: that your Father also which is in heaven may forgive you your trespasses.

❖ **Romans 5:3:** We rejoice in tribulations also, knowing that tribulations works patience and patience experience and experience hope; and hope makes us not ashamed because the love of God is shed abroad in our hearts by the Holy Ghost, which is given unto us.

❖ **Philippians 3:14:** …this one thing I do, forgetting those things which are behind, and reaching forth unto those things which are before, I press toward the mark for the prize of the high calling of God in Christ Jesus.

❖ **2 Corinthians 4:8-10** We are troubled on every side, yet not distressed; we are perplexed, but not in despair; persecuted, but not forsaken; cast down, but not destroyed; Always bearing about in the body the dying of the Lord Jesus, that the life also of Jesus might be made manifest in our body.

❖ **Psalm 139:14:** I will praise thee; for I am fearfully and wonderfully made: marvelous are thy works; and that my soul knoweth right well.

Chapter 2

Abuse & Self Esteem

Healthy relationships have respect, trust, communication, acceptance, loyalty, safety and consideration for each other. Sadly, lots of relationships do not have even half of those, and many turn abusive. Abuse is not love and it is your responsibility to stop it or remove yourself from it when you see even the slightest sign of it emerging in any way. You must believe that you are worth much more than to have someone abuse you in any kind of way. Period. Point blank! If the person that you are involved with does not bring out your best qualities then you do not need to be with them. If you find yourself in a relationship where you are the one constantly giving, constantly providing for, putting forth all the effort, going over and beyond, and always trying to make things right, then you are in a one-sided relationship. A relationship should not be that hard. It should be reciprocal, not unilateral. The person that you have chosen as a partner should bring out your best qualities, not your worse. This person should enhance your life, not take away from it by creating misery and unhappiness in it. When there is a situation where one feels uncomfortable, having to walk on eggshells, never feeling at ease or at peace around their so-called partner, then they may be in an unhealthy or abusive relationship. There are many forms of abuse and they are all wrong. Some people tend to think that if their partner is excessively jealous, it means that they love them. Many think that this jealous mentality is cute. Jealously is a major red flag and there is nothing cute about it. People have gone into violent rages and committed murders because of jealousy. Is that cute? There are various forms of abuse, although physical abuse is the most common and the most discussed since it is the most visible, but other forms of abuse happen every day and includes sexual, psychological, financial, and believe it or not, religious abuse. Below are brief descriptions of each just so you have an idea of what it looks like in order to avoid it or do something about it if you see signs of it in your life or in the lives of others. You may even need to look at this list in order to face what you may be doing to another person. If you see yourself as the abuser/aggressor in any of these categories, then get some help. You are reading this book for a reason.

Physical Abuse - Inflicting pain onto another person via hitting, slapping, pushing, shoving, punching, choking, kicking, hair pulling, dragging, biting, tripping, cutting, stabbing, shooting, etc.

Sexual Abuse - Forced and unwanted sexual acts upon another person without their consent via rape, incest, molestation, oral sex, anal sex, fondling, fingering, foreign objects, etc.

Psychological/Emotional/Mental Abuse - The infliction of verbal mental or emotional anguish upon another person using words including threat, humiliation, demeaning, manipulating, scaring, lying, interrogating, condemning, persecuting, intimidating, isolating, blaming, brainwashing, etc.

Financial Abuse - Any act that affects the material security of another person against their wishes including, irresponsible use of money, gambling, financial risk taking, excessive spending, employment prevention, demanding an explanation of all money spent, stealing money, hiding money, not permitting spending for necessities, abusing or manipulating credit cards or loans in another's name, and/or demanding another's paycheck.

Neglect - Deliberately withholding necessities, essentials or needed items from another including, food, clothing, money, care, love, affection, toiletries, etc.

Religious Abuse - Using a religious book to make a person feel unworthy, sinful, guilty, or dirty; using religious teachings to manipulate others into performing unholy or ungodly acts; to intimidate by preaching "righteous indignation" or making others think they are going to hell by twisting the religious teachings to justify their own actions and/or using scriptures to condemn.

If you find yourself in any of these situations, then something needs to be done right away. It is *your* responsibility to create a safe and abuse-free environment for yourself. Unfortunately, some people have been abused so much that they begin to think that it is normal. There is nothing normal about a person feeling demeaned, worthless and inadequate. There is nothing that you or anybody can do in a relationship that justifies any kind of abuse. If you are being abused or feel the need to abuse another person in any kind of way, then you do not need to be with that person and should immediately disconnect yourself from them. Abuse is about control. An abuser needs someone to abuse or they feel less of a person. There is always an underlying cause for both the abuser and also the victim who allows themselves to be abused. Abusive relationships exist because of the psychological makeup of both parties involved, not just the abuser. Hurt people hurt people. In other words, people who have been hurt, most times end up hurting others.

Whenever someone says or does something hurtful, there is always a root cause beneath the surface; but this does not mean that you, being the victim must make allowances for his or her abuse and justify their actions. This is also not a reason for you to justify yourself staying with them. Although there is an underlying reason that a person abuses, it does not mean that it is your job to discover that reason. When abuse is discussed, we typically think of men as abusers because they are statistically more abusive than women, but some women have been subject to abusive behavior as well. It is important to note however, that women are more likely to suffer physical and sexual abuse than men. More often than not, when women abuse, it is usually verbally and psychologically.

Relationships become abusive for several reasons. An abuser seeks to make their partner feel inferior in order to make themselves feel superior. By demeaning their partner, the abuser feels a great sense of control. Psychological and emotional abuse can be hard to detect and even harder to cope with. Those who have been abused emotionally have a hard time trusting people and are often timid. Abuse is not love. When someone loves you, they do not hit, demean, or criticize you. They do not advertise your shortcomings and faults to make you feel worthless, then later says, "I love you." An abusive relationship is a dysfunctional relationship. Love makes you feel happy, secure, appreciated, comfortable and free. Abuse is not love.

THE EFFECTS OF LOW SELF-ESTEEM

Self-esteem refers to how you feel about yourself on the inside. The thoughts and feelings you have regarding yourself may be positive or negative. The more positive your thoughts and beliefs about yourself are, the higher your self-esteem will be. On the contrary, the more negative your thoughts and beliefs about yourself are, the lower your self-esteem will be. Feeling good about yourself is imperative, because it gives you a sense of power over your own life, helps you feel content in relationships, allows you to set realistic expectations, and enables you to pursue your *own* goals. Notice I said "own" goals. I place emphasis on this word because it is very important. One main characteristic of those with low self-esteem is that they go over and beyond to help others achieve their goals and seldom work on achieving their own. They do this so that they will be accepted, so people will appreciate them, recognize them, like them, and praise them for their efforts and hard work. Yet, they leave their *own* goals and dreams on the backburner and never get around to pursuing them because they are constantly helping others fulfill theirs. Feeling great about yourself gives you the motivation required to achieve goals and reach your dreams. Feeling bad about yourself on the other hand, contributes to a distorted view of who you are and gives you a distorted view of others. The limitations that you think you have, and the negative thoughts that you internalize are given to you by the world, but the possibilities that you envision for yourself come from within you by the spirit of God residing in your soul. Ralph Waldo Emerson states, *"What lies behind us, and what lies before us are tiny matters compared to what lies within us."* What a profound statement! There is so much greatness within you. Therefore, in order to be great, you must first believe that you are great, expect great things and be ready to receive them when they arrive.

THE CONFIDENCE TO BE YOURSELF

A major characteristic contributing to the quality of your life is confidence. With confidence, you pursue your goals and dreams with boldness. With confidence, you tackle life's challenges with the faith that you will overcome each one triumphantly. Confident people "know" that they are important and they believe that their lives matter. They make a difference in this world. They go out and make things happen. They are fully aware both of their strengths and weaknesses and they tackle their weaknesses in order to strengthen them. Without a doubt, people who develop goals and diligently work at accomplishing them, get more achieved with self-confidence than without it. They walk in this world with assurance in the things they know how to do and the openness to learn the things they need to learn. These are the leaders of our world, the movers and shakers of their industry, the doers of great things. Self-confidence is a hot commodity because everybody wants it, yet people envy those who have it. It compels people to you. Men are attracted to women who are self-confident, independent, and have self-respect. Men are not attracted to women who are timid, self-doubting, insecure of themselves, needy, too emotional, desperate, or too dependant upon others. Men cling to women who are confident, free and empowered. The self-confident person does not go overboard to impress others, but is confident in who they are and pursues their own goals. People have always been drawn to those who do their own thing without worrying about who is scrutinizing them, talking about them, or who dislikes them. Their confident demeanor draws others to them. This is because self-confident people have qualities that everyone admires. The confidence is in their walk, their talk, their conversation and their behaviors.

I have noticed that when it comes to confidence, one's appearance often does not matter because their confidence supersedes everything else about them.

When a woman acts like a prize, a funny thing happens: the man forgets what she looks like because her magnetism is so strong. People are drawn to those who have self-confidence because they want it too. No normal person is drawn to a person with low self-esteem regardless of how beautiful or handsome they may be on the outside. People with low self-esteem seem to go overboard trying to make other people happy instead of seeking their own inner joy and happiness. If something or someone can make you happy, that person or thing can also make you unhappy, and that is way too much power to give to someone else over you. Those with self-esteem issues overcompensate and there is no challenge in being with them because they are constantly withdrawing from others to the point that it becomes draining because of their dependency. You do not need to seek approval from others. The only approval you need is God's approval. Be the type of person who pours into the lives of others in a positive way, not constantly draining them. True confidence comes from knowing that you are worthy and deserving of the things you desire and through self-reliance, you pursue those things. There is no way that you can be internally self-confident if you allow yourself to be abused. That is totally contrary to what self-confident people stand for. If you want to know what is inside of you, look at what is outside of you. Look at what is around you. You

31

have drawn these things to you. You have brought them into your experience. Sometimes this discovery can be a bit painful because you must see what you have created in your life. Sometimes the discovery can be liberating and reassuring when the things around you are pleasant, harmonious and prosperous. What's on the outside is a reflection of what is on the inside.

Adopt an attitude that it is impossible for you to fail and recognize that success is inevitable because you deserve it and are worthy of it. If you do fail, you must know that what you failed in, was not meant for you at that time and then continue moving forward. You must believe and know that God and His universe are on your side. Everything goes back to your beliefs, thoughts, and words. One of the biggest causes of low self-esteem is the thoughts you hold in your mind about yourself on a daily basis, which supports your low self-esteem. Make sure that the thoughts you entertain are not negative and self-defeating, which minimizes your self-worth. Practice self-confidence on a daily basis. The following are some things that you can do to practice being confident:

- Be assured in your conversations and give eye contact. Don't look elsewhere when talking to people. Look them in their eyes.

- Be clear and convinced when speaking to others. Know what you are talking about and convey your knowledge in a self-assured way.

- Walk with your back straight and your head held high. Typically, people with low self-esteem walk a little slower than most people and often keep their heads looking down at the ground. A head that is held high is a sign of self confidence.

- Initiate conversations when it is appropriate to do so. Introduce yourself to people and engage in positive discussions.

- Dress in a manner that says you are important. Stay well-groomed and neat.

- Speak out when it is necessary to do so (only when it's necessary).

- Never let anyone mistreat you. Stand up for yourself.

- Do not compromise your integrity. Hold on to your morals. Always be ethical and remain honest.

With self-confidence, you draw a different caliber of people into your life. You begin to feel good about yourself and your thinking process changes for the better. Practice confidence and your fears and insecurities will soon vanish. You are not other people's opinions of you. It does not matter what has been spoken over you or who has spoken them. It doesn't matter what happened in the past. The past is gone and there is no bringing it back. You become what you believe. If you have accepted negativity about yourself and are believing that you are anything less than a prince or princess of God who is worthy of prosperity, success, grace, honor, and greatness, then you need to reevaluate the beliefs about yourself. Anything that you believe that is contrary to who God says you are is a lie! God says in 2 Peter 2:9 that you are, ... *a chosen generation, a royal priesthood, a holy nation, a peculiar people; that ye should show forth the praises of him who hath called you out of darkness into his marvelous light.*

Get the lie out of your belief system. Get it out of your conscious and subconscious mind. You can do this in many ways.

- Create an affirmation, which is a statement affirming who you desire to be, but written in the present tense. As you repeat your affirmation, the constantly repeated words sink

34

into your subconscious mind and the subconscious mind begins to draw all the elements that will make you into the person you decree you are.

- Listen to motivational CDs that feed your self-esteem and remind you of the fact that you are a powerful person filled with great possibilities and potential.

- Read the Bible, which is a book of life. God's Word reminds you of your self-worth and reassures you of the power that you posses within.

- Change your conversation to speak only positively. Never let anything come out of your mouth that you do not want to see manifested in your affairs.

People are looking at you and wondering if you truly believe in your vision, your goals, and your dreams. If you are not positive, if you are not confident, if you are not excited about your OWN goals, how can you expect anyone else to be excited about your goals? When you work with diligence towards your dreams, people notice, and they will support your vision. Everything you do will make an impression on others, good or bad. Therefore, it is of the utmost importance that you begin to value yourself as a person worthy of accomplishing great things regardless of what has happened to you in your life.

One with a low self-esteem stemming from abuse or other things does not recognize their inner strength and fortitude to develop goals and pursue them with persistence and unwavering faith. Think about it. Is it characteristic for a person with low self-esteem to believe in himself or herself and pursue their goals? No, it is not. This person is too insecure and deep down inside they believe that they are not worthy enough to be great, although they may dream of greatness. If one asks for success, but prepares for failure, they will get what they have prepared for. Confident people prepare for great things everyday. What about you? What are you preparing for?

People who allow themselves to be abused do not look for gifts inside them because they do not believe they are worthy of having any God-given gifts; but you showed up on this planet with a seed of greatness inside you and when you were born, your possibilities were endless. There is greatness in everyone, but not everyone embraces their greatness. Some feel that because of the things they have endured, there can not be anything good awaiting them in life, but understand that the things you endured are

36

directly connected to your divine assignment. They are the very things that make you great. Great people have amazing stories of trials and challenges to tell. They have been through some major struggles, but they persevered, overcame, and refused to be taken captive by self-pity, poverty, or bitterness. Thomas Edison was born with normal hearing, but when he was just a boy, he was a candy butcher on trains. One day a man lifted him and his candy up onto a train by his ears. That was the beginning of his deafness. After that incident, he could have lived his entire life with anger and bitterness about what was done to him, but instead, he found the good from that situation. After he eventually lost his hearing completely, someone asked him, *Do you see your deafness as a great handicap?* He responded by saying, *To the contrary. Deafness has been a great help to me. It has saved me from having to listen to a lot of worthless chatter, and it has taught me to "hear from within."* Now, that is what I call finding the good out of the bad. In addition to that, he found his greatest power, by learning to hear from within. We all must get to a place where we can "hear from within." After all, that is where the spirit and power of God resides - within you. When we can hear from within, we hear God's voice speaking to us ever so clearly. And when we can resonate on what He says, we will find that nothing else matters. All that matters is what He says about you.

37

Oprah Winfrey is another example. We all know who she is. Oprah is one of the most powerful, richest, influential women in the world, but her life did not start off that way. She had her internal struggles of feeling worthless, meaningless and devalued because of the sexual abuse she endured as a child. At nine years old, and living in Milwaukee, Oprah and her siblings were left with their 19 year-old male cousin to watch them. It was this cousin who sexually abused Oprah for the first time. She was raped and then taken out for ice cream while told to keep it a secret - and she did. She was abused again some years later by a family friend and then again by an uncle some years after that. She kept this ongoing abuse silent for many years. Many women are still struggling with sexual abuse experienced by one person, but can you imagine being abused by three different people on three different occasions? Only God knows how this child felt about herself, the world and men in general.

Evidence suggests that the negative psychological impact of child sexual abuse persists over time, often into adulthood. Potential long-term effects of sexual abuse include depression, anxiety, Posttraumatic Stress Disorder (PTSD), sexual dysfunction, and substance abuse. Further, among the female adult outpatient population, individuals with sexual abuse histories as children were twice as likely to attempt suicide than their non-abused counterparts.

Across the lifespan, individuals who were sexually abused as children are four times more likely to be at risk for developing a psychiatric disorder and are about three times more likely to abuse substances than their non-abused counterparts. It is estimated that approximately one third of child sexual abuse victims experience PTSD as adult survivors. Among women whose abuse involved penetration, an increased risk associated for the development of PTSD is experienced. Since children are less inclined to express themselves appropriately, their shame, frustration and worthlessness is manifested in different ways: misbehaving, withdrawal, depression, etc. Oprah does not deny that she experienced these feelings and often talks about the devastating effects that those experiences had on her as a child, teenager, adolescent and young adult; but she did not let those experiences keep her down. In spite of her dark secrets, she gravitated to the goodness inside of her. She took hold of her gifts, talents and abilities and used them to achieve worldly success. When the opportunity presented itself, she used those painful experiences to help others who have been abused. Can you imagine if Oprah would have held on to the bitterness, shame, disappointment and worthlessness and allowed those negative feelings to keep her down? The whole world would be different. Can you even imagine a world without Oprah? Thomas Edison and Oprah Winfrey are only two examples of people who have endured very difficult experiences in their lives. Were not these incidents considered emotional baggage? If not effectively dealt with, these two people could have lived their entire lives in misery, bitterness, unhappiness and regret, but they didn't. In spite of what their past contained, their inner strength and fortitude would not allow them to live in negativity. Because of these strong resolves, the world is a better place. And so I say to you, in spite of what has happened, know that you are not alone. Sometimes the worse your situation seems to be is an indication of the size of the reward that you will receive for having endured and overcoming. Nothing comes to stay. Things come to pass and they always leave a valuable lesson behind, a spiritual nugget of wisdom.

There are some things that can happen to you that will bring you to your knees in desperation and seemingly despair; but how you overcome those tragedies determine the degree of greatness that will be produced in you. Until you find your purpose and let the gifts that God has placed inside you flourish, you will never be great. The only way to live a rewarding and fulfilling life is to spend time with God in prayer. You cannot be fulfilled without accomplishing what God has ordained for your life. *...be filled with the knowledge of His will in all wisdom and spiritual understanding.* (Colossians 1:9-10). Winston Churchill said, *"To each there comes in his or her lifetime a special moment when they are tapped on the shoulder and offered the chance to do a very special thing, unique to them and fitted to their talent. What a tragedy if that moment finds them unprepared or unqualified for that which could have been their finest hour."* The more you pray, the clearer His will for your life will become. Until then, you will have a void and will constantly search for that feeling of contentment, fulfillment, and peace that passes all understanding that only God can give. Les Brown, a national motivational speaker is the epitome of how one who had a strong will to be great, a motivation to be successful, a desire to overcome other people's negative predictions, and a strong unwavering faith in God will bring you to the point of surmounting even your highest expectations. In his book, 'Live Your Dreams', he quotes, as it relates to gifts and talents, the following: *"Most people never nurture their gifts, skills and abilities. Each of us has a unique offering. No one else is going to produce your product, write your book, open your academy. And if you don't bring your gift forward, if you die with it inside of you, then we will all suffer from being deprived of your particular genius."* He further writes, later in the chapter the following: *...the richest place on the planet is not some diamond mine or an oil field. It is a cemetery, because in the cemetery, we bury the*

41

inventions that were never produced, the ideas and dreams that never became reality, the hopes and aspirations that were never acted upon. How sad. Most people die never having shared their gifts with the world, thus never being fulfilled. Don't let your dreams die within you. Let them blossom in your lifetime. The feeling of completion, accomplishment, and gratification will not emerge until you complete that, which you and only you were created to do. There is nothing worse than starting multiple tasks and not finishing any of them.   When you start things and never finish them, you are operating in a spirit of incompletion and failure. Your subconscious mind gets into the habit of not completing.   When you scatter your efforts, you cannot expect to succeed.

God seeks expression through us and He expresses Himself through men, women, and children. The variation of gifts we have are all for God. He wants mouths to sing beautiful songs for Him and to speak His truths. He wants hands to play beautiful music for Him, to draw beautiful pictures for Him and to build magnificent skyscrapers for Him. He wants eyes to behold his beauties and to experience His miracles. He wants to express Himself through you because it is Him that enjoys all these things.   Most people have many gifts, but we all have at least one. The key is to take your particular talent to a level where it has never been taken before and you can only do that when you believe in yourself. With the gifts you have been given comes the responsibility to use and develop them. Keep your effort on the areas where you shine. Some of the things other people find boring will actually energize and enrich you if it is your gift. Find your God-given gift. Cultivate it. Nurture it and use it for the glory of God.

SCRIPTURAL NUGGETS

❖ **Proverbs 18:16.** A man's gift makes room for him, and brings him before great men.

❖ **2 Corinthians 6:14:** Be ye not unequally yoked together with unbelievers: for what fellowship hath righteousness with unrighteousness? and what communion hath light with darkness?

❖ **Philippians 4:13:** I can do all things through Christ who strengthens me

❖ **Galatians 5:22-23:** But the fruit of the Spirit is love, joy, peace, longsuffering, gentleness, goodness, faith, meekness, temperance: against such there is no law.

❖ **1 Corinthians 15:33:** Be not deceived: evil communications corrupt good manners.

43

Chapter 3

Dating & Communicating

Dating requires openness, acceptance, and communication, especially if you are at a point in your life where you are transitioning into new phases and trying to figure out exactly what those new phases will be. Unless you are already in a mutually exclusive and healthy relationship, then trying to date while undergoing the inner healing process may be a difficult thing to do. Dating can be a pleasant experience or it can be complicated depending on how you go about it. Some people casually date, meaning that they go out with different people socially for the fun of it. They have no ties, emotional or otherwise to any one person, so they may be with someone different every other week. This may work fine for some as long as they are up front with the individuals they are casually dating and are being responsible about it.

MOTIVES WHEN MEETING

I often hear women talk about how they want a man with money. They look at how he dresses, what kind of car he drives and what kind of job he has in order to determine how much money he *may* have in his bank account. Women use this as a measuring stick to make a determination of whether he has money to meet her needs or not, and she decides whether to give him the time of day. It is amazing how some women want men with money when they don't have any themselves. It is important for women to understand that when meeting a man, if your motives are not right from the beginning, you will be the one hurt in the end. You may get the man with the money and you may get the lifestyle you want for a while, but sooner or later, your wrong motives will come back to haunt you. When you go into a relationship with wrong motives, your heart isn't right; and you will eventually reap what you sow. I am not saying that you should not have standards, but what I am saying is that if you refuse to date a man because of what you see he has not yet acquired materialistically, then your heart is not right. This man could be your soul mate and with your help could evolve into a great man who will eventually make millions, but you will not allow yourself to even converse with him because of what you see he does not possess in the natural. The sad part about all this is that some of the women I hear talking about what a man has to have in order for them to date him are themselves broke, living from paycheck to paycheck with jacked up credit. You want a man to have acquired so much and you yourselves are not living up to the standards you require for your future mate. What are you bringing to the table besides your good looks, fine body and good sex? How much money is in your bank account?

When I talk about dating, I refer to meeting someone you have an interest in, then getting to know and learn that person mentally, intellectually, and eventually romantically. Different cultures have different practices on dating, but in the United States, dating usually starts out as a friendship, or at least it should start out that way. It typically begins with two people who are physically attracted to each another. The initial conversations usually determine whether future conversations or interactions will take place between the two. If so, then the conversations become frequent. Each dialogue gives you an indication of how the person thinks, rationalizes and behaves, although conversation alone is only a small indication. Sometimes it only takes two minutes for you to realize that the person you are talking to does not have it all together mentally. Stop it right there because if you don't, it will become a problem later on down the line. Some men, when they realize that a woman is a little flaky, will try and sleep with her first and then drop her after that, but my grandmother always said, *"If you find them dumb, leave them dumb."* Don't take something from people first, then drop them. That is using them and what goes around comes right back around. On the other hand, you might meet a person who you are attracted to and discover that they seem pretty decent and appears to have their head together. That is a good sign. Keep in mind though, that most people put their best qualities out front when they meet people for the first time. It is common sense. People are pleasant, kind, friendly and sometimes complimentary. They seem to have interesting conversation and some are very charming. Friendships on all levels begin this way. If people showed that they were moody, judgmental, critical or abusive, nobody would ever want to get to know them better, so people put their best qualities out front. Keep this in mind when meeting people, because we all do it.

With dating, the attraction to each other evolves into a more serious friendship as you and the other person share interests and begin to desire the companionship of each. When your interest to each other becomes strong to the point that neither of you have any desire to date other people, it then becomes exclusive, which means that the dating transitions into a relationship. This decision is agreed upon by both individuals. As the relationship progresses, you continue learning about each other. You continue being interested or begin disliking the characteristics that are beginning to surface through them. If things are going good, you start to really care about them and are pleased with their personality traits. In the first instance however, you must make a decision of whether you want to continue trying to make it work even when you are starting to notice things about them that you do not like. If their bad qualities outweigh their good qualities, then it is not worth it for you to continue trying to make it work. I have always heard that when a person shows you who they are, BELIEVE THEM. They could not act that way if it were not in them to be that way. If they act crazy and out-of-control one day, you'd better believe they will act crazy and out-of-control again.

Learning and getting to know each other is foundational in dating. It is an ongoing process that does not happen quickly. As time goes by, more of the real person is revealed and various situations will show you their true colors, how they respond to stress, whether they have integrity, how they treat other people, how they manage their finances, etc. The process takes time, and as it unfolds, you come into a new revelation of who they really are. You also discover a lot about yourself as you are learning them. Also keep in mind that as they reveal who they really are, your actions are revealing who you really are to them. Just as you are learning and observing them, they are also learning and observing you, and if you react to their actions negatively, they will view you negatively, regardless of the reason *why* you responded the way you did. Either way it goes, the relationship will move forward and the way in which it evolves determines your next move. This is why it is not a good idea to marry someone you have known less than six months. I have heard of people getting married after only knowing someone for three months. This is a bad idea! The in-love feeling has not worn off yet in three months. Therefore, your perceptions of the true nature of the person is not yet clear. Three months does not give you enough time to find out their true character. At least you would have seen and learned a whole lot about someone in six months, but my suggestion is to date at least one year. That way, what you see in a year is pretty much what you are going to get going forward. Some people fall in love and immediately want to get married because they are thinking from the "in-love" feeling, not realizing that the "in-love" feeling is going to wear off and reality will set in. What is the rush in getting married so soon after meeting someone? If you think that he or she is "the one" then date for at least six months and see if you still feel the same way after that. What is the rush in marrying right away? Allow things to transition naturally, good or bad.

Human nature causes everyone to desire love, affection, and validation. There is nothing wrong with giving your heart to a person and allowing a person to give you theirs, but there are no guarantees in love and love does not come with a warning disclaimer. Just as you want someone to handle your heart with care, you must handle the heart of the one you hold with care as well. Falling in love is a glorious feeling. Falling out of love is a frustrating and sometimes uncomfortable feeling, and experiencing a broken heart is a devastating experience. Although each of those emotions feel differently, it is healthy to have experienced them all because they each will contribute to making you a stronger person. You will be able to encourage and uplift someone else who will cross your path one day and will need the wisdom from your past experiences; but the only way that you can help another person is if you have experienced what they are going through yourself and you were able to handle it appropriately. Otherwise do not attempt to help someone else because you will end up exacerbating their situation instead of helping them get through it. The key is to effectively deal with the painful experiences of your past. Do not let them take root in your heart, mind, and soul becoming emotional baggage. Move forward with confidence and assurance that your relationships, be it friendships, family, or romantic, will be positive and healthy, and if they are not, it will not be because you sabotaged them.

COMMUNICATION

Communication is an absolute must in every area of life that deals with people. It is the sole means by which information is shared. The clarity of the information conveyed determines the degree of understanding to the receiver. When it comes to dating and relationships, communication is the avenue by which individuals are effective in understanding each other's thoughts and feelings. Poor communication skills, disagreements and misunderstandings can be a source of resentment and distance which can ultimately lead to an ugly breakup. Without communication, a relationship will inevitably fail. It is important that both individuals are able to effectively communicate their thoughts, feelings and concerns to each other without fear of being criticized, insulted or offended. In all interaction with people, we should use communication to establish a common ground in order to understand each other's points of view. People in relationships need feedback from each other. Without it, they will not know what the other person expects. Relationships usually deteriorate when what is needed and wanted is not expressed or communicated effectively.

As the relationship gets more serious, conversations on not-so-comfortable issues must be held. For instance, if marriage is being considered, then money matters must be discussed. Raising a family, where to live, and how many children to have are also necessary conversations. One may notice that the other has a major problem with shopping too much and not paying their bills on time. This is a red flag that their financial priorities may not be in order. These issues would need to be addressed if both parties are assessing each other's suitability as a future spouse. The amount of debt that has been accumulated by each is vitally important because if marriage is being explored, then the debt that one has becomes the debt of both. Is it fair for the responsible person to be penalized by having their credit damaged because of the irresponsibility of the other? When you get married, everything becomes one, so if one has bad credit, then two people's credit becomes ruined as opposed to the one. This is also why credit score conversations should be held as well as savings and spending habits. Look at what each of you are bringing into the relationship. If marriage is seriously being considered, then everything needs to be reviewed. In other words, do an assessment of what is being brought to the table: I have a car; he has a car. Check. I have my own place. He has his own place. Check. (shows responsibility) I have been on my job for nine years. He has been on his job for 12 years. Check. (shows stability). My credit score is 716. His is 560. RED FLAG! I have $3,563 in my savings account. He has $139.16 in his savings account. RED FLAG! (Where is his money going?) As difficult and uncomfortable as it may be, these conversations must be held and you must decide what should be done about the bumps and hurdles. I certainly am not suggesting breaking up with someone because they have little money saved or because they have a bad credit score, but a conversation needs to take place and some decisions should be made.

Although many do not believe in pre-marital sex, over 80% of Americans who are sexually active are not married. Therefore discussions on sex and the manner in which each likes to be pleased should be held, along with the best safety precautions to take. When problems or disagreements about sexual issues are not discussed openly and honestly, it can bring stress and anxiety into the relationship. This is all a part of effective communication. Not nagging or badgering, but communicating in a mature, rational and understanding manner.

KEEPING THE FIRE BURNING

There are plethoras of books, magazines, online articles, blogs and chat rooms all over the world on dating, relationships, marriage, etc. These books are written because so many people seem to have difficulty keeping the romance and fire burning in their relationships. The fire is usually very hot in the beginning of a relationship, but at some point, it begins to dwindle until eventually it has burned out. I will not attempt to tell you that the advice I am about to present on relationships is the cure all to take or the guaranteed way to go when dating or in a relationship because people interact differently in their relationships and if what you are doing works for you, then why fix what is not broken? However, what I am going to share with you comes from a combination of personal experiences and advice given to me from those who have managed to experience trial and error and finally found what seems to work. After reading these tips, you will agree that they are simple, practical, sensible, but most importantly, they do work. Keep in mind that the advice is geared towards those who are on the dating scene, not married.

KEEP A MENTAL BALANCE. Don't be too nice and don't be too mean. A mental balance is always good. That is what keeps most men and women on their toes – that is, when a partner is not a pushover and will not hesitate to tell you how they feel within the parameters of respect and maturity. A "yes" man or woman is a turn-off and does not provide any mental or intellectual challenge to their partner. Surely, in a relationship, you will not agree on everything. If you disagree with something, you should convey your feelings in a mature, rationale and respectful way. When you concede in every disagreement however, it can be frustrating to the other person, especially when they know that your concession is not how you really feel. Everyone likes a little mental debate every now and then. But please do not be too contentious and contradictory about everything. There is nothing cool about that. In fact, that will run a person away.

BEING TOO COLD. Speaking as a Black woman, I know that we can sometimes be downright cold, mean, and even ruthless with our tongue at times; but men can also be that way. To a very large extent, this disposition is sometimes rooted in the childhood upbringing; in some cases, it is the absence of a father or mother; it can also be the result of past abusive relationships; a past broken heart; tumultuous mother/daughter father/son relationships and overall emotional baggage. In order to keep the flame in the relationship burning, we have to learn to let some things go, especially petty things. Every single thing does not merit an argument. Isn't it better to lose the battles and win the war in the end? Being cold and hard for too long becomes a turnoff and will eventually push the other person away.

DO NOT REVOLVE YOUR LIFE AROUND YOUR PARTNER. Have your own life outside of them. Pursue your own goals. When you are dating, your life should not stop and your goals should not be put on hold just because you have a companion. Your life should not revolve solely around the other person's schedule either. You do want to work them into your priorities if they are worth it, but allow him or her to miss you at times. Spending almost every available moment together becomes old very quickly. It does feel good in the beginning and can seem hard to be apart from each other, but it makes it all the more better when you are made to miss them and they you. Give space. Do not be so readily available all the time. You should have many other things to do than sitting by the phone waiting for your partner's call and then picking up on the first ring.

BE ACCEPTING OF OTHER PEOPLE. Everyone is different. We not only look differently, but we think and rationalize differently as well. Realize that others will not always see things your way. Yes it becomes frustrating when others do not see things the way you do, but you have to be able to accept other people's opinions and how they feel. Continuing to harbor upon your point of view and trying to drill your way of thinking into another's mind is a waste of time. *"A man convinced against his will is of the same opinion still."* It is an exercise in futility. Most times it is best to agree to disagree.

KNOW WHEN TO BE QUIET. Everyone hates a nagger. People who complain about everything and everybody turns others off. After a while, people tune you out and then make it their business to stay away from you as much as possible until they find a way to leave you altogether. There is a time to speak and a time to be quiet. When you have gotten your point across, but are still talking too much, cut it off. Shut up. Give it a break! There is nothing positive about monopolizing a conversation, not allowing anyone else to speak, and then going on and on. It is even worse when no one is listening anymore but you are still yapping away.

DO NOT HOLD GRUDGES. I was the queen of this. If you did one remotely bad thing to me, that was it. You were cut off and our friendship or relationship was over. I lost so many friends this way; but with wisdom, I have learned to forgive others when the hurt they caused me was not intended to be malicious or spiteful. Sometimes people do the wrong things, but with the right motives and there are other times when people do the right things, but with the wrong motives. When it comes to your relationships, if a friend or partner has hurt you, but you have decided to stay with them anyway, then you must sincerely forgive and then release what they did to hurt or betray you. You may not forget it immediately, but you can choose not to talk about it. What is the purpose of staying with someone when you are going to keep reminding them of the wrong they did to you every time there is a disagreement? Where is the good in that? No, it is not easy to forgive right away, but constantly bringing up what they did will keep the pain alive and fresh. You will never be healed of it as long as you keep pouring fresh energy into it by talking about it and harboring on it. However, after you have addressed the issue with them and explained how the situation made you feel, if you decide to forgive them, then make up in your mind to never bring up what they did again. You will soon find that eventually, the hurt will be a distant memory and the thought of it will no longer cause you pain.

BE SPONTANEOUS. Spontaneity does not have to mean a weekend Vegas trip. It does not have to cost money. This could mean a bouquet of roses sent for no reason; a beautiful card given just because; an "I love you" e-mail out of the blue, a bottle of cologne or perfume just because, etc. These are ways to keep the fire burning in the relationship.

PRAISE YOUR PARTNER. We are created in the image of God. He desires praise and worship from us and we desire it too. Nothing feels as good as having the apple of your eye give you praise. This is the one main secret to keeping a mate. Men, like women do desire praise from their woman as well. They will not tell you that though, but they love it when their woman shows her appreciation for their manhood in the

59

relationship. Women often fail to realize that. Men need validation as well. Praise is good every now and then. It lets your partner know that their efforts are not going unnoticed and they are appreciated. But to extend the praise a bit more, you should find his or her passion and praise them right there. That is when it really has a meaningful impact.

DON'T LET HIM/HER STAY OUT THERE FOR TOO LONG. When your partner has done wrong and you have decided to put him or her out, or you decided to leave in order to teach a lesson, do not stay out there too long or do not let him or her stay out there too long. If you know that you only packed up and left or put them out to prove a point, then make them work their way back home or work to bring you back home. If you let them stay out there for too long, or if you stay out there too long, either one of you may begin to enjoy your newfound freedom and lose the desire to reconcile. There are many single people who are ready to pick up your man or woman and do all the things that you failed to do. If your mate has done wrong, but you still love and want them, then teach the lesson, and let them come back home or teach them the lesson and you go on back home.

I actually saw the devastating results of what happens when a couple is separated too long. She and her husband were seemingly doing okay in their marriage. It wasn't utopia, but it was fine. They have three sons, lived in a beautiful home together in the suburbs and both had decent paying jobs. Her husband reluctantly dealt with her not keeping the house clean and not cooking, but what he would not tolerate was her new habit of going out with single women to nightclubs. This was something that she had started doing and it really bothered him. She ignored his requests to stop and continued to dress up and go out with her friends to the clubs. He would constantly ask her why she felt the need to hang out with single women all of a sudden. He would tell her that those women were looking for what she already had: a good husband, a nice home, a family unit, etc. To make matters worse, she and her friends would take pictures with men at the clubs and she would post them to her Facebook page thinking that her husband would not see them since he did not have a Facebook account; but other people told him and he addressed that with her as well. Needless-to-say, many arguments ensued because of this issue. She would say that the men were just friends and that she was going to live her life. He would try and explain how inappropriate it was for a married woman to not only go to nightclubs, but take pictures with single men. He would say that it didn't look right and was disrespectful to him.

This one particular night, she got dressed to go out and her husband told her that if she went out that night, he would pack his things and leave. She got dressed and left the house anyway. He stayed there with the children until she returned and walked out the front door with his suitcase in hand the minute she walked in. He went to one of his fraternity brother's homes and told his wife that he would not be coming back until she could tell him that she would stop going out to the clubs. She refused and continued hanging out even after he had moved out. He continued coming to the house to pick up the children, taking them to their sports practices, going inside and watching TV when he would bring them home, and occasionally he would spend the night since he and his wife were still intimate. However, she made no attempt to change and he became frustrated and hurt. It became clear to him that she had no regard for how adamant he felt about the situation. She also seemingly began enjoying the freedom. After all, he still paid the bills, he still cleaned up when he came over, and they were still sexually active. She stated that she enjoyed not having to hear him complain about how untidy the house was and that the only thing she missed was his cooking, since he frequently made dinner. Now she had to cook for the kids. She never asked him to come back home and he never made an attempt to do so since she continued hanging out. They were separated for eight months until... he met someone else. Not only did he meet someone else, but he fell in love with the new woman. When I talked to him about not allowing the enemy to break up his family, he bragged about how totally opposite the other woman was from his wife, how clean, organized and ladylike she was and how structured she was with her own children. He bragged about how she cooked every night and packed his lunch for work each day. He boasted about how she liked to cuddle while they sat on the couch and watched TV - all the things his wife did not do. I noticed that when he talked to me about this woman, he glowed and he was genuinely happy. Of course, I didn't share this with the wife. I told her to pray and fight for her marriage, but her pride would not allow her to fight and she allowed the anger and bitterness to consume her. He stopped going inside the house when he dropped the children off home and he stopped sleeping with his wife. Needless-to-say, she found out about the woman and went ballistic, to say the least. I will not go into all the details surrounding that, but he told his wife that she should have known he had found someone else when he stopped sleeping with her and stopped coming inside the house after dropping the children off. Who would have thought the situation would have gotten this out-of-hand? All because she did not respect her husband enough not to go to nightclubs with single women when he asked her not to. She took for granted that her husband would come back home and take whatever she dished out. Now, she and her girlfriends are truly *all* single and *all* looking for the same things: a man. She let him stay out there too long. Eight months is a long time if you want someone back. They divorced eleven months after he moved out. He is still with the other woman and still seems to be happy. I learned a lesson while watching her go through this. I guess she never thought he would find someone else. Now she's hurt, devastated, bitter and angry. We must learn how to compromise so we can keep the relationship healthy. This is a true story.

Gary Chapman wrote a book entitled, 'The 5 Love Languages' which was primarily written for married couples, but the book applies to all couples as well. In a nutshell, he explains that every person has a specific love language that they speak and need to be reassured in. When their partner communicates to them in their specific love language, they feel appreciated and loved. The five love languages are:

1. Words of affirmation
2. Quality time
3. Receiving gifts
4. Acts of service
5. Physical touch

After reading that book, I definitely saw validity and credibility in what he explained. Realistically, if we look at the five love languages, we find that we do fall into one of these categories. Briefly, Gary Chapman described each as follows:

WORDS OF AFFIRMATION. These are words spoken to one's partner that shows their love, appreciation, gratitude, or attraction to them. Words may compliment, uplift, encourage, or praise their partner. If this is the other person's love language, then they feel a great sense of love and appreciation when they are complimented, told how much they are loved or are just told nice things in general.

QUALITY TIME. A person may feel that their love tank is being filled the more time they spend with their partner. When they take a vacation, go to the movies, eat out at dinner, spend time at a play or concert or just watching television together, it fills their love tank and makes them feel secure. These people are the ones who take the initiative to make reservations to the restaurant, plan the vacations, and find out what's playing at the movies.

RECEIVING GIFTS. This love language fills a person's love tank when they receive things. It could be flowers, candy, a new laptop, a poem, a giftcard, a nice bottle of cologne or perfume, etc. For the person whose love language falls into this category, their tank becomes filled when their needs are met in this area. It communicates to them that they are cared about when their partner spends time picking something out for them. These people typically have saved every card given to them; have the box to every gift and have every poem or letter saved from years ago.

ACTS OF SERVICE. As weird as it may seem, some people really feel loved when domestic services are performed around the house or in other areas. For instance, a man may love it when the woman cooks, keeps the house clean, washes and puts the clothes away on a regular basis, takes good care of the children, or irons his clothes. For a woman, it could be mowing the lawn, painting the guest room, fixing the garage door or taking her car for an oil change or service check.

PHYSICAL TOUCH. Although most men fall into this category, Gary Chapman suggests that a secondary love language be selected if this one seems to be the number one love language for a man. Because of his biological make-up, a man may think that this is his language. However, since men have a natural inclination to sexually release, they would probably choose physical touch not because it is necessarily their primary love language, but because of their need to release. However for women, physical touch may mean the need to hold hands or cuddle. This is not to say that women do not have the biological need to release as well. This is why if physical touch is selected as the first love language for either the man or woman, a secondary language should be chosen, just to be sure that all the areas are being covered.

Always keep in mind that everything that is seen has an unseen cause behind it. A child who may never have heard the reassuring words of 'I love you' from a parent or anyone else for that matter may have a need to have verbal reassurance in certain areas of his or her life. Hence 'words of affirmation' may be their love language when they become adults. In like manner, one who may not have received very many gifts growing up as a child, but desired them, may need 'receiving of gifts' as their primary love language. When we understand why people act or behave the way they do or have certain expectations, then we can meet them at their needs. More often than not, we do not know why people behave the way they do. Sometimes they themselves do not know why they behave the way they do. People may see things a certain way or feel the need to be loved in a specific way but do not know why. The reason could be so buried in their subconscious mind that they do not even know it, but just like emotional baggage, it seeps out at the most inopportune times.

As I close this chapter, I will remind you that you only have one life and that life is so much happier and full of joy when you have fulfilling and peaceful relationships with people. This world can be a very lonely place without someone to share your life with. When it comes to your mate, you want to ensure that your relationship (married or not), is a fulfilling one that enhances you as a person, contributes to your joy and peace, provides your life with a nice balance and an occasional mental challenge. Knowing and understanding yourself can help you to learn and understand others.

SCRIPTURAL NUGGETS

❖ **2 Corinthians 4:18:** While we look not at the things which are seen, but at the things which are not seen: for the things which are seen are temporal; but the things which are not seen are eternal.

❖ **Romans 12:18:** If it be possible, as much as lieth in you, live peaceably with all men.

❖ **Galatians 5:22-23:** But the fruit of the Spirit is love, joy, peace, longsuffering, gentleness, goodness, faith, meekness, temperance: against such there is no law.

❖ **Ephesians 4:29**: Let no corrupt communication proceed out of your mouth, but that which is good to the use of edifying, that it may minister grace unto the hearers.

❖ **James 1:19**: Wherefore, my beloved brethren, let every man be swift to hear, slow to speak, slow to wrath:

Chapter 4

Intimacy, Love & Sex

The desire for romance is rooted in the psychological makeup of both men and women. Intimacy is a closeness that two people share in a relationship that is developing and progressing. Intimacy is not sex. They are separate, although intimacy may lead into sex. Dating inevitably progresses into romance and intimacy. After two people have spent considerable quality time together while enjoying a mutual adoration and attraction for each other, then intimacy comes into play. Intimate relationships play a necessary role in the overall human experience. This stage allows couples to express their emotions in a physical manner by way of holding hands, hugging, massaging, fondling, kissing, cuddling and making love. It makes both individuals feel good physically and emotionally and allows the affectionate part of who you are to be expressed. Intimacy should not be confused with love though. In other words, you do not say you love a person because of the way they make you feel physically. Sex is not love. Love is not sex. Sex and love make a good combination, but one is not inclusive of the other. Romance sometimes fades. When this happens, there must be something worthy about the person that you can hold on to. When there isn't anything admirable, praiseworthy or commendable about the person, then what you probably have is lust, not love. However, because you may already love a person, the love may make the sex that much more pleasant; but when you confuse love with how a person makes you feel during sex, your perceptions of the true essence of the person become distorted and all you see and focus on is the physical satisfaction they give you while at the same time, overlooking essential characteristics about them that are important, such as character, integrity and values.

When God created the world, He made male and female to comfort and give each other companionship. Prior to this, Adam was not satisfied being alone. Although God gave him dominion over all the animals and he had everything he needed in the garden of Eden, he still was not fulfilled. There was still a void in his heart. It was not until God created the woman that the void Adam felt was filled; and so it still is today. It is human nature to desire companionship, but you have to make sure that you choose the right companion. When you allow someone to come into your life just to be able to say that you have somebody, but the person you choose does not enhance you or make you better, you regret it at some point later on. When you lower your standards and compromise your expectations because you are tired of waiting for the "right person", you often bring stress and frustration into your life. Sometimes it is better to be alone and at peace than to have someone in your life who brings frustration and disappointment to you.

Just as God took a rib out of Adam and placed it in his woman, He has done the same for you. If you are a woman, He has placed the rib from the man He created just for you and put that rib inside of you. If you are a man, He has placed your rib inside of the woman he made just for you. Now, it is up to you to make the choice to allow that man to be your Adam or that woman to be your Eve. I know that you are asking, *"How do I know when it's him or her?"* God will reveal it to you when you pray, live holy, and walk in receptivity to His leading and guiding. No, it is not easy, but if you are a woman, you are not to go looking and searching for your husband. That is the man's job to search for you. The Word says, *"He who finds a wife finds a good thing."* It does not say, she who finds a husband... It is the man's job to search for a wife not vice versa. The woman's job is to prepare herself for marriage. Stay pure. Pursue your goals. Go to church. Fast. Pray. Read your bible. Keep yourself holy. Socialize with your girlfriends. Get your finances in order. Work on inner healing so that when the man of God does appear, he will not have to spend most of his energy trying to peel back layers of hurt, pain and emotional baggage left behind from past relationships just so he can get to your heart.

I repeat, the Word says, *whoso finds a wife, finds a good thing.* (Proverbs 18:22). It doesn't say, *whoso finds a 'woman' finds a good thing.* I point that out to say that just because a man has found a woman doesn't mean he has found a wife. Every woman is not a wife. She must already be a wife in her heart when he finds her. She must already know how to treat a man, manage the household, care for the children, etc. Men are finding women and marrying them, but they are not finding wives. This is why men are disappointed after getting married and discovering that the woman they married is loud, unladylike, cantankerous, emotionally unstable, irresponsible, doesn't know how to talk to or treat him, doesn't regard the Lord or the Word of God, unwise and unlearned. Men, you can get any prostitute or crack head on the street corner and make her your wife. Does that mean you have found a "good thing?" No, because these women are not wives. You may also find a woman in the church who attends every Sunday. This too, does not mean that she is "a wife" nor does it mean that she is born again. *You shall know them by their fruit* (Mathew 7:20). Below are some signs that will tell you if you have found yourself a wife.

- She puts God first in her life

- She has a strong prayer life
- Studies the Word and applies it to her life
- She carries herself like a lady at all times
- She is strategic with her words and she lets no corrupt communication proceed out of her mouth
- She interacts with people in a pleasant manner
- She manages her anger with calmness and maturity
- She knows how to communicate without yelling and screaming
- Others admire, respect, and look up to her for guidance
- She keeps a clean house and has structure in her household
- She has positive relationships with her family members
- She has standards and values and is not afraid to communicate them

So men, keep in mind that when finding a "wife" these are some things you need to look for because every woman is not a wife!

MULTIPLE SEX PARTNERS

Sexuality is a part of the human experience, but it is neither wise nor safe to have multiple sex partners, even when using condoms. Males tend to do this more commonly than females because for most males, the sex is purely physical. Many men do not need to have an emotional connection to their sex partner in order to have sex. Sex for some is purely a physical act and has nothing to do with love. For a lot of men, they do not have to love nor like the person they have sex with. The act is purely for the physical gratification it gives. Having various sexual partners for some people is not a big deal. Most women however, do need to have an emotional connection to their partner when having sex and tend to have their hearts and feelings involved; but there are some who have been hurt so much that they feel they are not worthy of respect or honor and they turn to sex just to feel good physically. Inwardly, they know that what they are doing is wrong, but the devil speaks to their mind, constantly reminding them of their past, telling them that they are worthless, and they believe the lies. As a result, they seek out men to give them physical gratification, but the gratification is only temporary. However, the hurt, pain, void and worthlessness they feel is permanent until they find the source of their healing. Until then, they go through men to experience that momentary feeling of being wanted. As long as you have not dealt with the painful experiences of your past, you, in your own strength will not be able to fill the void you feel. When you lean to God and give Him all your hurt, He heals and delivers you completely. No man can give you the peace and joy that God can.

I do not advocate fornication. I promote and suggest holiness through abstinence, but I know that this is an area that many single Christians struggle in; and for this reason, I suggest that for safety and moral reasons, you choose one sexual partner and choose that person wisely if you have not yet been delivered in this area. If you choose to have sex, then seriously think about being monogamous. What is *monogamous*? It means seeing, dating, courting, being intimidate with, or having sex with only one person for an extended period of time. It means that you are that person's only partner and that person is your only partner. You significantly reduce the risk of acquiring an STD when you are monogamous. However, this does not mean that a condom should not be used during intercourse. Even if birth control pills or other contraceptives are used, they only prevent pregnancy, not STDs. If you want to go the route of not using condoms with your monogamous partner, you may want to consider getting a physical examination and an HIV screening and ask your partner to get one as well, then show the results to each other before making this decision. Whatever way you decide, just make sure you decide responsibly so you will not have to worry about treating a curable or even worse, an incurable STD because of being sexually irresponsible.

SEX TRANSMUTATION

Abstaining has many advantages. The first time I ever saw the word *"Sex Transmutation"* was in Napoleon Hill's book, 'Think and Grow Rich'. If you have not read this book, I suggest you do so. It is for individuals who are ready to achieve their goals, master their minds, obtain massive success, and organize their lives by capitalizing on their gifts, talents and abilities. It is also for those who are ready to activate the seeds of greatness within them and take that greatness to a level that they never dreamed of. The book is only for those who are ready to take their lives to the next level through diligence and hard work. The meaning of the word *transmute* is, *"the changing, or transferring of one form of energy into another."* In his book, Napoleon Hill states that sex transmutation is:

"the switching of the mind from thoughts of physical expression, to thoughts of some other nature. ...when driven by this desire, men develop keenness of imagination, courage, will-power, persistence, and creative ability unknown to them at other times. So strong and impelling is the desire for sexual contact that men freely run the risk of life and reputation to indulge in it. When redirected along other lines, this motivating force maintains all of its attributes of keenness of imagination, courage, etc., which may be used as powerful creative forces in literature, art, or in any other profession or calling, including, of course, the accumulation of riches."

What essentially is being said above is (for those not married), if you take the desire that you have for sexual release and allow that desire to be transformed into creativity, ingenuity, and originality, you will see powerful manifestations appear in the conditions of your life. The transmutation of sex energy requires great will-power but the reward is worth the effort. The desire for sexual expression is inborn and natural and should not be suppressed or eliminated. It should be given an outlet through forms of expression that enrich the body, mind, and spirit of a person. If not given an outlet through transmutation, it will seek outlets through purely physical channels.

Sex desire, *"may be submerged and controlled for a time, but its very nature causes it to be ever seeking means of expression."* (Napoleon Hill). If the sex desire is not transmuted into creative effort, it will find a less worthy outlet. The emotion of sex contains the secret to ingenious ability and the person who has discovered how to turn sex energy into creativity and ingenuity has lifted himself to the status of a genius.

Being wise means using good judgment in every area of your life. You are the controller of your destiny and the choices you make today will determine the outcomes that you will face tomorrow. If you choose to have sex and you are not married, then be responsible and use precautions. If you could visit the HIV-AIDS unit at a local hospital, you would be shocked at the number of young people, teenagers, adolescents, and also senior citizens who are fighting against the disease. HIV-AIDS is one of the most if not the most severe STDs in the world. There are other STDs that are incurable as well and can be just as deadly as HIV-AIDS, especially if left untreated. Being health conscious means being responsible and balanced in mind, body and spirit.

OXYTOCIN
Oxytocin is a hormone that is produced by both males and females. It is released by the body when

intimate touching is exchanged. Kissing, caressing, fondling, and other sexual stimulation will lead to the secretion of oxytocin. In turn, increased levels of this chemical will lead to a cascade of events involved in sexual arousal and orgasms. This chemical is released by the pituitary gland in the brain and is referred to as "the love potion" or the bonding chemical because it is responsible for bringing people closer together during sex. When released, this chemical makes you feel calmer, less aggressive, relaxed, and more open and honest. Oxytocin plays a vital role in human emotions.

When this chemical is released from one person, it is picked up by the other causing both to feel a sense of closeness to each other. During sex, however, the increase in oxytocin causes a woman to bond intensely with her partner, creating romantic and emotional attachment. However, about the only time a man experiences a surge of this chemical is during an orgasm, which allows him to reciprocate the bonding during that time as well. But after his orgasm is over, a man's oxytocin levels usually return to their low states while the woman's levels continue to remain high. This is why a man may be compelled to say, "I love you" during sex, but may not feel like saying it much afterwards when the woman is longing to hear those reassuring words of love and affection from him. But of course, this is not the case with a man who cares for or loves his female partner.

81

Oxytocin can also spread through the air and be inhaled by others. As soon as a person releases it, it can be picked up by another person. Normally, the level within a body is low, unless there is a strong chemistry between people. When your body gets a little extra oxytocin, you will feel a slight wave of euphoria. You feel calmer and more at peace. You will also be more approachable and friendly. Higher levels of oxytocin in women enable them to be good mothers to their children and respond to the emotional needs of her spouse and her friends. Oxytocin also plays an important role in childbirth and lactation. It causes the muscle contractions that push the baby down the birth canal and the pulses that push breast milk toward the nipples. For this reason many people think that only women produce this chemical, but as you have just learned, that is not true. It is released during sexual orgasms in both men and women.

It is no big revelation that intimacy and romance play a huge part in relationships. Romance is what keeps the fire burning, but needless-to-say intimacy and romance alone can not carry a relationship. It should be an enhancement to other qualities that hold a relationship together. And then of course the responsibility of sexual intercourse should always take precedence over sexual stimulation because one should never lose sight of what is in the best interest of their health. It is a beautiful thing when you finally connect with the person who adds to your life in a positive way, one who keeps you laughing and supports you when you are down. When you finally are with someone who enhances you as a person, the intimacy is all the more delightful, but keep in mind that a relationship is hard work. It will not run on autopilot. Both parties have to be willing to put in the work needed to keep the motivation in the love tanks full. When you learn your partner's love language, you are in a better position to understand them and meet them in that area. Love can be a beautiful thing, but it takes work. However, the effort is worth the reward.

SCRIPTURAL NUGGETS

❖ **1 Corinthians 6:19:** What? know ye not that your body is the temple of the Holy Ghost which is in you, which ye have of God, and ye are not your own?

❖ **1 Peter 1:16:** …it is written, be ye holy; for I am holy.

❖ **Genesis 2:21-22:** And the LORD God caused a deep sleep to fall upon Adam, and he slept: and he took one of his ribs, and closed up the flesh instead thereof; And the rib, which the LORD

God had taken from man, made he a woman, and brought her unto the man.

❖ **1 Corinthians 6:13:** …Now the body is not for fornication, but for the Lord; and the Lord for the body.

❖ **2 Corinthians 4:16-18:** … though our outward man perish, yet the inward man is renewed day by day. For our light affliction, which is but for a moment, worketh for us a far more exceeding and eternal weight of glory; While we look not at the things which are seen, but at the things which are not seen: for the things which are seen are temporal; but the things which are not seen are eternal.

Chapter 5

When the Heart is Broken

It has been said throughout the ages that love is the strongest force in the universe. People have many different definitions of what they perceive as love and it is also a term that is used very loosely. However, when it comes to matters of the heart, one thing is for sure: **No one can tell you what you feel in your heart!** Falling in love is one of the most beautiful feelings there is and it is even greater when it leads to marriage. Although many have tried, you can not help nor stop who you fall in or out of love with. Falling in love happens so gradually that you do not realize it until the day it hits you that you are actually in love! There are signs that may indicate that you are falling in love and it is okay, although it can be a little scary. The one main thing that a person in love really fears is that the love will not last. They fear what will be replaced if the feeling of love leaves. That is a legitimate concern, but it should never be a reason not to allow yourself to be loved or to love another person with all your heart. Allow love to unfold naturally, because that is when you experience the fullness of the essence of love. If you are in denial and want confirmation that you are in love, look at the list below and see if you find yourself doing these things. If so, you may be IN LOVE!

- Smiling because you are thinking about the person or something they said or did
- Constantly wondering what he or she is doing
- Have an intense desire to talk to them frequently
- Programmed a special ring tone in your phone for them
- Wishes the call was them every time your phone rings
- Visualize yourself married to them
- Imagine what your children will look like
- People say that you are glowing
- Can not concentrate on your work
- You miss them when they are not around
- You have a great deal of respect and adoration for them
- You have flashbacks of the last intimate time you had with them

The feeling associated with being in love is a beautiful one and can turn into something very meaningful and long-lasting. When you open yourself up to receiving love, you get the beauty of the most powerful force there is and when you give the same love in return, you experience the gratification that comes with giving your heart to another. However, there are times when the feeling and emotions are not reciprocated. That is when rejection comes in to play.

REJECTION

The other side of falling in love is rejection. It can be the worst feeling in the world when the object of your love does not feel the same way about you anymore as you feel about them. A feeling of rejection followed by feelings of embarrassment sets in and is sometimes replaced by sadness and depression. Rejection does not feel good at all. It is a demeaning feeling that causes you to feel inferior and sometimes unworthy, but it is a phase of life that everyone should experience in order to learn and grow. Getting rejected teaches you to be strong as well as how to appropriately deal with others who you may have rejected so you can understand how they may have felt. Men, women, and children want to have their love returned more than anything. Being rejected does not always have to do with you and you should not allow your self-confidence to suffer because of it. You can

87

not control how another person responds to you. It could just be your season to experience what this particular emotion feels like. The person who rejected you was just the unlikely vessel used to bring it to you. The most important thing that you should know about rejection is not to allow it to take root in you. At some point, you will have to get up and say to yourself that although that person may not have wanted you, there is someone out there who does. Getting rejected simply means that who or what you were rejected by was not meant for you. Point blank! We all experience various emotions at different times in our lives. These emotions are necessary in order for us to be balanced, well-rounded humans. Happiness, joy, excitement, love, inspiration, sadness, anger, frustration, discouragement, and rejection are the basic human emotions that people experience during their lifetime. The sadness, anger, frustration and rejection do not feel good, but the happiness, love, excitement, and joy sure does. We have to experience them all in order to be balanced. There is no reason to get upset with the person who you feel rejected you. They should not be condemned for feeling the way they feel or not feeling the way you think they should feel. If their feelings for you do not parallel your feelings for them anymore, then obviously they were not the one for you. This is no reason to put up a wall and not allow yourself to open up to a worthy person again and be loved in the future. You must move in the confidence and assurance that your rejection will be replaced by full and complete acceptance from someone else who will love you unconditionally.

FALLING OUT OF LOVE

Unlike falling in love, falling out of love is not a good feeling. It is hard when the person who was once the apple of your eye is now someone you barely think about or someone who no longer has the same adoration and love for you. This does not mean that something is wrong with either of you. This happens all the time. Sometimes people who fall in love end up staying together for a very long time, and others end up falling out of love and going their separate ways. It happens. Some of the signs that may indicate that you are no longer in love may include:

- Forgetting to call
- Ignoring your partner's calls
- Little desire to spend time with them
- Getting off the phone quickly
- Little motivation to talk to them
- Not interested in going out anymore
- Getting irritated from small things they may do or say

When these things begin to happen, the relationship should be analyzed by both individuals and a decision on whether to stay or part ways should be made. Most times, this is no one's fault. Time could just have grown you apart, which reveals that the person is not your soul mate. There is nothing wrong with making the adult decision to go your separate ways after you both agree that the relationship is not working out the way you thought it would or should be. In some instances though, both parties are afraid of making the first move for whatever reason, and stay together for the sake of not being alone. Some feel that it is better to be in a miserable relationship than to be alone. This decision only wastes time and prolongs the inevitable. Breaking up does not have to be a complicated or bitter deal. It can be made by two mature, level-headed adults who can either remain friends afterwards or completely sever all ties with each other.

It is important to remember that just because the in-love feeling is over does not mean that the relationship should end. The in-love feeling does not last forever. It is a temporary euphoria that lasts no longer than two months. If you know that you have a quality individual who enhances your life, respects you, clearly cares for you or loves you and has your best interest at heart, then if the feelings are mutual, you should not break up just because the in-love feeling has passed. If there is something left to hold on to after the in-love feeling and after the sex, then hold on to that person. Good people are hard to come by.

The nature of women is to talk things out. That is how we were made. Most women are rational, emotional creatures who like to get to the bottom of things. We want closure. Men on the other hand generally are more withdrawn when it comes to talking about things bothering them and they only withdraw more when women try to drive it out of them. Men tend to internalize and do not like to be forced to talk. This can be very frustrating for a woman who knows there is something wrong, wants to talk about it, but can not get a response out of her man. Men sometimes act this way because they do not have the courage to tell the woman that they no longer want to be in the relationship, so they deliberately behave in passive-aggressive ways in order to force their woman to break up with them. That way, they get what they want, and they will not be blamed for the break up. Please note that I do not stereotype all men when giving these examples because there are always those who are the exceptions, but for the most part, this is usually the way it is. Sometimes men are confused as to whether they want to remain in the relationship and they are trying to sort out their feelings. On the one hand, they do care for the woman and she does have some good qualities, but perhaps her bad qualities outweigh the

91

good ones. He is trying to decide if it is worth it to stay. Until that time, he may appear withdrawn, but when he comes to a conclusion, trust me ladies, you will know it.

A BROKEN HEART

A broken heart is usually the result of one person no longer having the same feelings they had in the beginning of the relationship and expresses a desire to break up. In my first book, *Destined for Great Things* (2007), I wrote the following as it pertained to the root cause of my broken heart:

"As I look back and reflect now, I realize that I was not hurt because I loved him so much. I was hurt because of the rejection. If he and I would have reconciled and I would have broken up with him again, I would have been just fine, but since he was the one who rejected me, that was a devastating blow to my self-esteem, self-confidence, and self-worth."

Falling in love can sometimes end up in a broken heart for the person whose feelings have not completely diminished. In almost all relationships, there is usually one person who loves the hardest and this is usually the person who ends up getting hurt the most. The person who loves the least always has the upper hand because they are very much aware of how much they are loved. The one who loves less has the most power. It is sad but true. As long as they do not take the other person for granted because of this, then it is fine. For this reason, your life should never revolve around another person. However, a broken heart sometimes has nothing to do with the other person but everything to do with you, your pride, your ego, and most importantly, your season. It is amazing how one person can have such a powerful stronghold on your life when you were perfectly fine before you met them. Some people can change your life so dramatically simply by ceasing to be a part of it. That is too much power for one person to have over your life. I have often heard the saying, *"It is better to have loved and lost than never to have loved at all!"* Only until you experience loving and losing someone can you fully appreciate the meaning of the saying. The experience of enduring a broken heart is an intently deep and painful thing to go through, but it is something I feel everyone should experience. It is a severe emotional pain that makes you feel like your heart is on fire and the flames just keep burning with seemingly no end in view. When you are heartbroken, you feel as though you can not go another day. You may wake up crying and go to bed crying. You put on a fake smile all throughout the day, but you are deeply torn apart on the inside. I have been there twice. That kind of pain is nothing to take lightly, but it does eventually make you stronger. In spite of how you may feel, you must know beyond a shadow of a doubt that the pain does go away. As with all other emotions, a broken heart only comes to pass, but it must run its full course, and you have no alternative other than to let it run its course. A broken heart is accompanied by other emotions that are all rolled up into one severe pain. All these emotions are in full force while your heart is broken. Those emotions include rejection, sadness, depression, and discouragement. If you experience a broken heart, you need to talk to someone about it because it is at this time that the enemy plays with your mind. You are vulnerable so he feeds on your vulnerability. He will even tell you to commit suicide so that you won't have to feel the pain anymore. For this reason, you should not go through it alone, you must get your feelings out; otherwise, suppressing those feelings makes you feel worse. If you do not have anyone to talk to, then a therapist or counselor would be helpful in getting you through it. Never call the person who broke your heart. You will only feel worse after calling them. If they do not want to be with you, then you can not get them to change their mind by making them feel guilty or sympathetic for you. Every time you call them, you will feel worse and will have to go back to square one and start the healing process all over again. As each day passes, you get stronger. Time is your best friend during this time. Let the process run its course. That is the only way you will get something out of the painful ordeal.

When God created us, He made men physically strong and He made women emotionally, mentally, and psychologically strong. Therefore women can and have endured a lot of mental anguish and heartache, and although the cause of the woman's pain oftentimes comes from men, those same men more often than not, can not endure half the pain that women can endure; but men get broken hearts just like women do. There are plenty of men who have buried themselves under their bedspreads for days as a result of their broken hearts. They have cried in the privacy of their homes and have loss their appetites too. When dealing with a broken heart, you must be able to talk about it while you are in pain and cry as much as you need to. Someone who has been through it is the best person to talk to. I promise that the pain does go away and you are a much different person when it does. When you can finally walk away from something that once hurt and caused you pain, and you have no more ill feelings about it, then it no longer has power over you. This means that you have been healed. What you walk away from determines what you walk into. If you walk away from someone who clearly was not the one for you in spite of how much you think they were, then you may just walk into the life of someone else who could be your soul mate. The funny thing about having a broken heart is that when you have completely healed from it, you see clearly. When you see the person again, the one who was the cause of your broken heart, you may wonder what you ever saw in them in the first place. You may no longer be attracted to them and see them with a different set of eyes, 20/20 vision this time. The key to being completely healed from a broken heart is to be able to fully love again and also allow yourself to be loved. The sad thing about the whole broken heart situation is that many people lock the doors of their heart and do not allow anybody else in for fear that they will get another broken heart. They pick up emotional baggage and hold on tightly to it. They say that in love there are no guarantees, but if you never go forward optimistically and open-minded, when will you ever find true love?

SCRIPTURAL NUGGETS

❖ **Proverbs 3:5:** Trust in the Lord with all thine heart; and lean not unto thine own understanding. In all thy ways acknowledge him, and he shall direct thy paths.

❖ **Psalm 34: 18:** The Lord is nigh unto them that are of a broken heart; and saveth such as be of a contrite spirit.

❖ **Romans 12:9:** Let love be without dissimulation. Abhor that which is evil; cleave to that which is good.

❖ **Romans 13:10:** Love worketh no ill to his neighbor: therefore love is the fulfilling of the law.

❖ **Romans 8:28:** And we know that all things work together for good to them that love God, to them who are the called according to his purpose.

Chapter 6

Awakening to a new Reality!

Y ou only have one life and it is up to you to live your life with the joy, peace, happiness and harmony that God has ordained for you. Or you can live your life with hurt, pain, unforgiveness, bitterness and anger from the things that have happened to you in your past. Bad things happen to good people, but the way you choose to handle the bad things will determine the quality of the lessons learned and the blessings that you will receive from enduring such things. The severity of your test is a good indicator as to the size of the blessing that is forthcoming afterwards. Look at yourself as pure gold. The more you put gold through fire, the purer it becomes. Each time it goes into the fire, more impurities are removed. It is the same with you. The longer you are in the fire, the more impurities are taken out of you. No matter what happens to you, you must persevere. God has given you inner strength and fortitude to overcome anything that comes your way. The story of your life on earth has already been written out from beginning to end. You may not know what that story is, but God knows and He will always guide and direct you towards the right path that is in line with your story and your glory; but once you see the path, you must walk it. It is important to understand that God does not force you to do anything. He has given you free-will and self-choice. For instance, He will not pick you up and place you on the path that leads to the unfolding of prosperity and success. He shows you the path, but YOU have to choose to walk it or not. You have great wealth on the inside of you and God shows you your value; but God Himself will not pay you. YOU must go within, recognize your worth and then pay yourself. God prepares the table before you, but YOU choose what to put on your plate. There is nothing that can or will happen to you along this journey of life that God has not allowed, but He has already equipped you with unlimited power, spiritual strength and great fortitude to handle everything that comes your way. All power is within you. The kingdom of heaven is within you, therefore the power to overcome any obstacle, challenge, or adversity is within you too. You can and will triumph over any bad situation if you recognize and use the power within you, which can only be found through seeking God.

It is written in the book of Jeremiah Chapter 1:5, *before I formed you in the belly, I knew you and before you came forth out of the whom, I sanctified you and ordained you...* The world starts your life with a birth certificate and ends your life with a death certificate, but if God says that He *...knew you "before" you were in the womb,* then you had an existence before you came on earth and you will continue to have an existence after you leave earth. Your spirit is eternal. Your flesh is carnal. You are a spiritual being having an earthly experience. This means that you are spirit. You already know that God is spirit. For this reason, we worship Him in spirit and in truth. He breathed His spiritual substance into you and you became a living, breathing, spiritual soul. Therefore, the essence of who you are is spiritual. Your body is not who you *really* are. Your body is only a coat of skin made of dust to contain your spirit until it is time for your spirit to fly away - out of that coat of flesh. Since you are spiritual, you must seek spiritual answers for your problems. The spiritual is superior to the natural. Natural things are temporary. Spiritual things are eternal. The answers to all of life's problems are found in the spirit and are also outlined in the Bible through the inspired, spiritual Word of God. The spiritual world is invisible to the natural eye and is quiet and unseen, but very powerful and always operating. The most powerful forces in the universe are invisible. Your most powerful forces are invisible too, but you can tap into your forces through silent meditation and communion with the spiritual part of your being.

101

The story of your life includes the trials, tribulations, hardships, difficulties, victories, successes, accomplishments, and triumphs. In order to be victorious, it is necessary for you to go through the hills and valleys, mountaintop experiences, wilderness experiences and also the Calvary and Golgotha experiences. When you are able to say like Paul:

Not that I speak in respect of want: for I have learned, in whatsoever state I am, therewith to be content.

I know both how to be abased, and I know how to abound: every where and in all things I am instructed both to be full and to be hungry, both to abound and to suffer need.
I can do all things through Christ which strengtheneth me. (Philippians 4:11-13)

then you will understand the scripture in Romans 5:3 that says, *We glory in tribulations also, knowing that tribulations worketh patience and patience experience and experience hope; and hope maketh not ashamed because the love of God is shed abroad in our hearts by the Holy Ghost which is given unto us.* Remember that life is about how you respond to your tests and trials, and not the test and trials themselves.

We have to play the hand that we are dealt with. We are not all born equal. We are all born free, but not

102

equal. Some are born with a silver spoon in their mouths and go home from the hospital to their family's mansion. Some are born into poverty and go home to the two bedroom section 8 apartment with seven other children and little food. Some grow up to become great men and women in the world; others end up with consecutive life prison sentences given to them from their teenage years. Their whole life is gone. Some have children who are born mentally disabled and will require assistance for the rest of their lives and some develop sicknesses that they themselves have to treat for the rest of their lives. Regardless of what shows up in our lives, we must play the hand we are dealt with. We have no choice.

I have a friend who was dealt a bad deck of cards, but she is playing her hand well. In fact, through her story, I learned a great lesson about unconfessed sin. She is the sweetest person one could ever meet. She is humble and meek and just a ray of sunshine. She shared with me that she and her husband were writing a book together; and of course I offered my services to help them in any way I could. She sent me the file to review and give my feedback on formatting, editing, proofing, etc. I briefly looked at the title and knew the book had something to do with marriage. However, when I finally had the time to sit and give the book my attention, I noticed that the title read, *For Better or for Worse: A Married Couple Living with*

AIDS. I was initially shocked and didn't know what to think right then. This was my friend and all this time I did not know what she had been living with. The first thing that came to my mind was that her husband had the disease and she didn't. Needless-to-say, I read the entire book. They had married when she was in her early twenties and he was a few years older. Out of the marriage, they had three children. He committed adultery and gave his wife HIV. She never knew that he had cheated until he was diagnosed with HIV and had no choice but to confess. It has been nine years now (as of this writing) and they both are living with full blown AIDS. While reading the book, there was something that really stood out to me, and that was when the husband talked about "unconfessed sin". In sharing his story, he explained that prior to marrying, he had been caught up into pornography and other sins that, "stunk in God's nostrils." He left his hometown and moved away, thinking that he was leaving all those sins behind to start a new life with his new wife; but since those past sins were never confessed, they followed him and manifested in his body in the form of AIDS. My friend is reaping the consequences of her husband's sins. She was a virgin when they got married. Did she deserve this? Who are we to say what we do or don't deserve? Did Jesus deserve the cross? My friend has to play the hand that she was dealt. She made the decision to forgive her husband and stay with him in spite of what he did; hence the title, *For Better or for Worse*. She loves him dearly, is good to him, and very submissive to him. This is the assignment she was given and she is fulfilling it with excellence. She is a remarkable woman of God and relies on her faith to sustain her. She says that whenever she goes to the doctor, she always gets the "bleak and grim" news, but she relies upon her faith in God to sustain her and she doesn't let the bad news get into her spirit to bring her down. She keeps a smile on her face and keeps it moving.

Unconfessed sin is very dangerous. We must confess before God every known and unknown sin with a repentant heart. It is written that, *Love covers a multitude of sins.* (1 Peter 4:8). Yes, there is a consequence for every sin, but once we confess our sins, *He is faithful and just to forgive us of our sins and cleanse us from all unrighteousness.* (1 John 1:9). Although there is a penalty for every sin committed, God will not allow that penalty to overtake you once you confess, because His love will cover that sin. Once you confess, the penalty has an expiration date. When David sinned, he always repented and went to God quickly. Although David had to endure the consequences of his sins, God always had mercy upon David. God will do the same for you and me. You must confess your sins - known and unknown. Unconfessed sin is dangerous!

There are so many women who have been sexually molested by family members, friends, uncles, stepfathers, biological fathers, brothers, etc. What has happened to the men who did these things? If they have never confessed their sins before God, there is a detrimental price to pay for such sin. Don't you think for one moment that the sin of molesting and raping will go unpunished! I don't care what it looks like in the natural, there is an effect for every cause. They will pay! This is why we do not have to hold on to unforgiveness towards those who have hurt or violated us because God said, *Vengeance is mine, I will repay says the Lord.* (Romans 12:19).

It is also important that we teach our boys about respecting girls and women. Boys are naturally inquisitive about the female body and from the ages of 10-20, their hormones are raging out of control. It is at this age, that many have molested little girls in order to experiment with sex. They have no idea of the detrimental damage they cause to the life of the child whose innocence they have stolen. This is the start of the emotional baggage of many girls and women. After the molestation, they tend to pick up more and more baggage and by the time they are grown, they are carrying a very heavy load. We must talk to our sons about what is right and wrong and how to control their sexual urges. Talk to them about sexual molestation so that they WON'T DO IT to anyone! Communication is the key. What is so sad is when the boys "experiment" at that age, many do not confess the sin. They think they will never get found out and they go on living their life thinking that all is well, but that unconfessed sin will find them out and come upon them as a violent anaconda and suck the very life out of them. It must also be reminded that little girls do grow up and they do remember and some of them will expose it when they are old enough, and they should! For this reason, I am adamantly against teenage boys babysitting little girls. I don't care how nice the boy is. If he is a normal boy, he is still inquisitive. We must use wisdom in all things. You do not predispose a little girl to a teenage boy or a grown man for that matter. We must also teach our girls how to carry themselves, especially around boys and men. I talked about boys from the ages of 10-20 experimenting with sex, but I did not address grown men who do this and there are many, many grown men who molest little girls, little boys and teenagers. All I can say is, may God have mercy on their souls!

TOTAL HEALING

When we clearly understand who we are in God through Christ, we begin to see the world and ourselves differently. When we recognize that we walk with a spiritual power that has no limits or boundaries, our lives change. When you can truly say and believe

107

in your heart, *For I am persuaded, that neither death, nor life, nor angels, nor principalities, nor powers, nor things present, nor things to come, nor any other creature shall be able to separate us from the love of God that is in Christ Jesus (Romans 8:38),* you begin walking in supernatural strength. Think this way: *"The enemy did not kill me because I am still standing and I know that I am valuable and worthy of great things."* When you think those kinds of uplifting, self-encouraging thoughts, you begin to attract a new set of circumstances into your life. The only way that total healing can take place is when you see yourself the way God sees you: divinely whole, complete, and perfect.

It all starts with a change in mindset. It is your mind that determines the quality of life. You are spiritual. Your mind is spiritual. Your mind can not be seen anywhere in your body because it is not natural. It is a spiritual gift that was given to you by God to shape and mold by positive and powerful thinking. The quality of the thoughts you put in your mind will determine your circumstances. Thoughts are things and they occupy space in your mind; so if you are constantly thinking about the terrible things that happened in the past, why it had to happen, how it has scarred you, etc., then you are filling up the space in your mind that could be occupied by positive thoughts such as:

Yes, I may have endured pain, disappointment, shame or guilt in my past, but I will not allow those memories to hold me back any longer. I seek freedom from the bondage of those events and the memories of them. They will no longer hold me hostage by taking residence in my mind and spirit. I will focus on forgiving others. I will forgive myself. I am God's child and He loves me and has forgiven me a long time ago. He desires my success and prosperity. I will work on achieving my goals. I will cultivate new ideas. I will accomplish great things. I will think on and work towards greatness, prosperity, peace, forgiveness and joy. I am valuable. I am a child of God and He loves me.

The point here is that your thoughts create your circumstances. Whatever you think about, you bring about and what you think about the longest becomes the strongest. Your thoughts are like magnets and they attract things into your experience; so if you know this, why not deliberately think upon things that are positive, uplifting, confident and beautiful? Why do you think that the scripture says, *...whatsoever things are true, whatsoever things are honest, whatsoever things are just, whatsoever things are pure, whatsoever things are lovely, whatsoever things are of a good report; if there be any virtue, and if there*

109

be any praise, **"think"** *on these things.* Jesus understood the power of the mind and the power of the spoken word. Start today to monitor your thoughts, and as a result, you will see that your life will change.

There is always calm before the storm and a calm after the storm passes. The turmoil and devastation comes during the storm; but the critical factor is what you are doing while you are in the middle of the storm. While in the storm, you should be praying, fasting, meditating, reading your Bible and drawing upon your inner strength. If you do this, then you will come out of the storm with great lessons learned, acquired wisdom, greater patience, and strength of character; not to mention an awesome testimony of God's glory! Remember that it is not what happens "to" you, but what happens "in" you that make the difference. You are more than a conqueror!

DIAMONDS FROM THE SCRIPTURES

❖ **Romans 8:28**: And we know that all things work together for good to them that love God, to them who are the called according to his purpose.

❖ **Matthew 6:33:** But seek ye first the kingdom of God, and his righteousness; and all these things shall be added unto you.

110

❖ **Jeremiah 29:11:** For I know the thoughts that I think toward you, saith the LORD, thoughts of peace, and not of evil, to give you an expected end.

❖ **Proverbs 3:5:** Trust in the LORD with all thine heart; and lean not unto thine own understanding.

DISCUSSION TOPICS FOR EMOTIONAL HEALING

1) Discuss the childhood memories that have caused you pain, rejection, or a low self-esteem. How has that affected you?

2) Analyze past hurt and disappointment and determine if they have had an affect on past relationships.

3) If you are an insecure or distrusting person of people in general, where do you think that came from?

4) How will you begin to release the emotional baggage that may still be resident within you?

5) Why do you have a problem forgiving those who have hurt you? Who does your unforgiveness hurt more, you or the person you are not willing to forgive?

6) Do you think you expect too much from your mate? Are your expectations unrealistic (analyze what they are before you answer)?

7) Do you rely on God for your healing or have you been searching for the void to be closed through the help of people?

8) Do you expect the opposite sex to make you happy, whole and complete? If so, do you think that is fair to them?

9) Do you resort to eating or shopping to make you feel better about yourself or your situation? If so, why?

10) Who does God say you are? Is it difficult for you to believe who God says you are and walk in that truth?

ABOUT THE AUTHOR

Dr. Merritt is the author of eight self-help, personal development, motivational books that compel individuals go within themselves to find not only the cause of their problems, but the source of their solutions. Most of her books are written from personal life experiences that are used to help others understand that troubles and tests are a part of life. She emphasizes that it is always about how you respond to such tests and trials that determines the degree to which you learn and grow.

Dr. Merritt is a Certified Keynote Speaker, Teen/Youth Facilitator, life coach, college professor and radio talk show host. She is one of only five individuals bestowed the honor of being named a 2011 African American Achiever recipient from JM Family Enterprises. She holds a Bachelors Degree in Elementary Education, a Masters Degree in Exceptional Education, a certification in Educational Leadership and a Doctorate Degree in Organizational Leadership with a concentration in Conflict Resolution.

Dr. Merritt travels the United States delivering keynote speeches addresses and teaching on various subjects of personal development. She is President/CEO of M&M Motivating (www.miamerritt.com), which provides services in teen/youth training, corporate retreats, conference speaking, seminars and staff development. She also writes online articles on various subjects and maintains a Wednesday's Wisdom Blog. To book Dr. Merritt for one of your events, please call **1-866-560-7652** or e-mail merrittmia@yahoo.com for more information.

Dr. Mia Y. Merritt
M&M Motivating & Professional Speaking
1-866-560-7652
www.miamerritt.com

Other Books by Mia Y. Merritt:
Prosperity is Your Birthright!
Prosperity is Your Birthright Workbook
Destined for Great Things!
Destined for Great Things Workbook
Words of Inspiration: Golden Nuggets for the
Wise at Heart
Life After High School
Life After High School Workbook
Editor of, No Glory Without a Story!
(written by a collection of authors)

www.ingramcontent.com/pod-product-compliance
Lightning Source LLC
La Vergne TN
LVHW011208080426
835508LV00007B/668